REVIEWS FOR

GENTLENESS:
It's Not What You Think

I am impressed by Ms. Henne's writings on 'gentleness.' Initially, she peeks around a corner with some trepidation to explore gentleness, at first for her children. She ends up inviting us into her journey, which expands and deepens into considerations from scripture in Greek and Hebrew. She continues our journey into questions of leadership, connections, self-control, kindness, humility, grace, and social connection. The path is deep and transformative. We end up sitting on the edge of our chair to discover what comes next. I am intrigued and changed. Thank you, Debbie, for this text that not only inspires but also challenges.

-**The Rev. Kittie Verdolini Abbott, PhD, CCC-SLP, MDiv.** *Professor, Communication Sciences and Disorders, University of Delaware*

***

Gentleness: It's Not What You Think is an engaging book concerning the most misunderstood fruit of the spirit. The book is full of stories that bring life to a biblical understanding of gentleness. Throughout the book are life-changing insights presented in encouraging ways. The depth of biblical interpretation also challenges persons who like to dig deep in the Word of God. The layout of the book provides a good resource for personal or small group study. It also provides easy to access concepts for sermon preparation on the theme.

-**Allan Yoder**, *Pastor, Good Shepherd Community Church*

***

I've known Debbie since she was a child. Our lives took different paths, but we have renewed our friendship after many years and enjoy regular contact. Who knew, indeed?! Debbie has a true gift in research and translating the complex into comprehensive and applicable information. She is a passionate young author who loves God with all her heart and knows Him intimately. The book is scattered with pertinent personal experiences that make for good reading, mixing the technical, intellectual, spiritual and practical. I have been around for a long time – I'm in my 80s as I write this – and have learned many things. This young woman has written the best definition and application of grace that I have heard or seen. The book is worth the read for that alone.

-**Marty Smith**, *Fivefold prophetess, intercessor, and speaker with DOVE International*

***

If you want to be a powerful godly leader, this book is a must read. In *Gentleness: It's Not What You Think*, Debbie Henne offers transparent insight from her experiences that both the young or mature Christian leader can glean. Whether your leadership is in the home, marketplace, ministry, or all three, you can learn, grow, and be transformed through the insights shared in this book.

I loved this phrase from the book, "Humility is not weakness, it's power's best kept secret." Whether you are looking for a simple teaching or an in-depth understanding on gentleness, you won't be disappointed. The research is trustworthy, the questions are challenging and award transparency. Doing this study alone or with others will help truly transform your relationship with God and others.

-**Deborah Davenport** *Founder/President. For His Splendor, Isaiah Sixty-One Ministry www.4hissplendorministry.org*

***

Gentleness: It's Not What You Think is very well written and has much needed leadership discussion. Gentleness is a fruit of the Spirit, but it is not talked about very much in our day. While we want to be strong leaders, gentleness is often associated with weakness and timidity. But Debbie shows the real strength that is required to be gentle. She skillfully uses original language to show the meaning of gentleness in scripture. She also includes research from other disciplines to show how important it is in our culture today. I think this book is very timely, being released at a time when we see a lot of angry opinions and general meanness in our culture which is revealing inadequacies, we have rather than strength. So this is a good time for us as leaders, parents, and citizens to consider why God places value on this attribute of godliness. I know everyone wants to learn how to be a stronger leader that increases influences, but gentleness is needed for this very thing. The book is a good read, very interesting, and will challenge in a helpful way.

-**Dr. Barry Wissler**, *President, HarvestNet International*

GENTLENESS

It's Not What You Think

DEBORAH HENNE

Published by KHARIS PUBLISHING, imprint of KHARIS MEDIA LLC.

Copyright © 2020 Deborah Henne

ISBN-13: 978-1-946277-71-8
ISBN-10: 1-946277-71-1

Library of Congress Control Number: 2020943678

All KHARIS PUBLISHING products are available at special quantity discounts for bulk purchase for sales promotions, premiums, fund-raising, and educational needs. For details, contact:

Kharis Media LLC
Tel: 1-479-599-8657
support@kharispublishing.com
www.kharispublishing.com

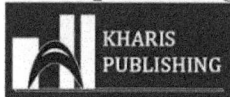

KHARIS
PUBLISHING

Dedication

To Randy, Rowan, Sierra, and Kendall who have provided unending love, support, and inspiration for me and this book.

CONTENTS

Foreword

We are honored to write this foreword for Debbie Henne's new book, *Gentleness: It's Not What You Think*. The title of the book says it all. Debbie has masterfully given us revelation of what genuine biblical gentleness really is and how to apply it practically to our lives. Many of the truths in this book were new for us as we read them for the first time. *Gentleness: It's Not What You Think* is filled with nuggets of truth, including some that you have probably never heard of before. Get ready to be surprised as you read through each page.

Jesus lived out true gentleness, and He calls us to do the same. This book is both scholarly and practical at the same time, a feat few author can accomplish. Expect to be challenged and changed by the truths and practical application found in the pages of this book.

In our current global environment, there is a desperate need for each of us to experience true biblical gentleness. This book will show you how to experience the gentleness of the Lord in your life each day. You will find this book to be a true gift as you experience the gentleness of the Lord minute by minute. Learn in these pages how you can deescalate arguments with others through the wielding power of gentleness and discover the revelation of true gentleness! You will never be the same!

Larry and LaVerne Kreider

Authors and founders of DOVE International

Preface

This book started out as a Bible lesson for my three daughters. At the time I began writing it, my oldest was in first grade. I decided I wanted to do a unit on the fruit of the Spirit, and, inevitably, we came to gentleness. Assuming I had the definition and the attribute down pat already, I decided I only needed to do some cursory prep for the lesson. However, I was shocked and humbled by what I learned. Rather than merely completing the educational unit with my children, I found myself reeling with fascination, and so much so, that that "cursory prep" turned into months of research. Learning how the Bible defines gentleness, and its impact on our lives and relationships, revolutionized the way I perceive myself and the way I approach interacting with others.

As God began to lay this book on my heart, I found a very serious struggle arising within me. I felt as if I wasn't worthy or qualified enough to write a book on this topic. I know how things can be perceived: you read a book by someone and assume that person is an expert in that area. After all, he/she wrote a book on it! If that is what you are expecting, you will be sorely disappointed. What you will find, however, are stories from my life sprinkled throughout the pages of this book. I try to be as honest as possible, sometimes painfully so. I share them with the hope that you will find encouragement and possibly some amusement from my blunders. You will see that, like you, I am a work in progress. I do not claim to have mastered my life, but I believe that as I continue to pursue the Lord, He will continue to work His character into my life...including gentleness.

Through gathering and compiling the information and resources found in this book, my goal is to inspire and challenge you to live a life of gentleness. But even if you don't feel up to a challenge doled out by a fellow human being, take heart, for this challenge is also God's and can be found in Colossians 3:12, where He tells us to clothe ourselves with gentleness. God never calls us to do something without empowering us, through His Spirit, to accomplish it. It is my prayer that reading Part I of this book will help you to better understand gentleness as the Bible defines it, and then challenge you in Part II to help you make gentleness a regular part of your wardrobe.

Acknowledgement

I would like to thank my parents for all of their love, guidance, and support. Thank you for teaching me how to live my life for the Lord, for always believing in me, and for helping me to believe in myself. I would also like to thank my cousin, Cindi Shantz, for encouraging me to complete this writing project over Christmas dinner one year. I do not believe I would have finished this book without your astute insights that helped me overcome my self-doubt. Each and every time I was tempted to give up, your words would pop into my head and give me just enough oomph to keep going. Last, but certainly not least, I'd like to thank those who provided manuscript feedback and support at the various stages of development: Mom, Kathy Lloyd, Amy Traffas, Elly Crist, Courtney Myers, Theresa Fidler, Dr. Barry Wissler, Dr. Katherine Verdolini, Pastor Allan Yoder, Marty Smith, Debbie Davenport, and Larry and LaVerne Kreider. Your contributions helped shape and polish the content of this book, and you will forever have my gratitude.

Redefining Gentleness

It's All Greek

Gentleness is one attribute that is, in my opinion, misunderstood and underestimated in our society. I'm sure we've all heard the expressions "gentle as a lamb" or "gentle as a dove;" both carry images of something soft, something fragile, something naïve and timid, and the association between gentleness and weakness permeates much of our culture. In fact, just a few months before I started writing this book, I was scrolling through Facebook and noticed that one of my friends was offended that someone had called her gentle. Her reason? She thought of herself as a woman of strength. I shot a quick reply to her post, encouraging her that I did not believe that gentleness and strength are opposites. I'm not sure she was convinced. However, according to the biblical definition, and despite what our culture suggests, strength and power are central to gentleness. So, while lambs are cuddly and doves are beautiful, I personally have come to think that lions are a more appropriate image for gentleness.

Lions and gentleness? Yes, you read that right. Lions and gentleness. Why would I choose a lion? Let's begin by looking at the original words used in the New Testament that were translated from Greek into English as "gentle" or "gentleness."

In the New Testament there are three different Greek words translated as "gentle." The first is found in the Beatitudes in Matthew 5:5, and this particular Greek word is translated as "gentle" in the New American Standard (NAS) version a total of four times in the New Testament. Jesus even uses this word to describe Himself in Matthew 11:29 when He says, "Take my yoke upon you and learn from Me, for I am gentle and humble in heart, and you will find rest for your souls." This word, *praüs*, is difficult to translate into English, and some Bibles actually translate this word as meek instead of gentle. Both words are associated in our culture with weakness but, when looking at the original, Greek definition of praüs, nothing could be further from the truth.

The first clue that praüs should never be associated with weakness is that it begins with God's limitless power. The second clue is that this power, according to *HELPS Word-studies*, is exercised under His control.[5] Notice, this word does not mean powerless, nor does it imply that this power is dormant or unused. *It is used* and, even more mind-blowing, this power is controlled. Imagine attempting to control even the smallest of earthquakes or the weakest tornado. Impossible, right? Well, God's power is even greater. Therefore, this word not only contains unlimited power, but also the ability to *control and use* that power without causing harm to the recipient. Remember my association between the lion and gentleness? The same powerful jaws that tear into and consume prey also carry their young. By their necks! What an amazing example of the concept of power exercised with control.

I'm not sure which is greater, the raw power itself or the ability to control and wield it. But before we begin to discredit and belittle the power involved in controlling and using that amount of power, we need to dust the cobwebs off our history lessons from grade school and remember dominant world leaders—Hitler, Stalin, and Napoleon come to mind. And all too quickly we see how the saying *absolute power corrupts absolutely* came to be so popular and timeless.[1] It is humanly impossible to control power of that magnitude.

Can people possibly possess this quality? According to Matthew 5:5 and 1 Peter 3:4, yes, we can. But how? The answer is as simple as salvation: through God's grace. God never calls us to achieve what is humanly possible, but He does ask us to stand in His grace through faith while He completes His work through us. As my mom always says, "God does not call the equipped, He equips the called."[7] I believe the way to remain uncorrupted by this aspect of gentleness is by understanding that it's not our power. We don't possess it by nature; we don't own it; nor can we even begin to wield it on our own. No, this power is God's and God's alone, and He chooses to use and equip us as vessels of His power, and *that* is humbling. Therefore, if we humbly stand in His grace and allow Him to work through us, I believe we can successfully avoid the pitfall of pride and have the privilege of seeing God work wonders before our eyes. In and of ourselves, we cannot control this type of power; but in faith we can trust that God will work His power through us and rejoice in the honor of participating in His great works.

Throughout the Bible, God uses the imagery of vessels to describe humanity (see 2 Timothy 2:21 and Acts 9:15), and I can't think of a more perfect illustration. The vessel is merely a tool used to transfer the substance inside. It is the substance within that possesses the desired qualities and power. A cup or bottle can't take credit for the power to quench thirst; all it can do is add flavor…and if it does, it's usually not very good! How ridiculous would it be to eat a clay jar or a cup to try to quench your thirst! We are the vessel, and God is the substance. It is our job to share Him with those around us with preferably as little flavor from our imperfect humanity as possible. After all, we can't take a scintilla of credit for quenching the spiritual thirst of those around us. All the power, the praüs, and glory is His!

The next Greek word translated as "gentle" in the Bible is *epieikés* and has a completely different meaning from praüs. This word was created from two Greek words, the first being *epi*, which we are familiar with thanks to words such as epidermis, epitome, and epiphany, and means "on," "over," and "near." The second word is *eikos*, which means "equitable" and "fair."[2] Keeping these word roots in mind, let's take a look at this word in context in Philippians 4:5.

In this letter, Paul and Timothy are writing to the church Paul founded in Philippi. As is seen in other letters written by Paul, he includes a list of instructions before concluding. When I read this passage, it appears that this list is divided between a mysterious "true companion" and the "rest of my fellow workers." In the portion that appears addressed to the true companion, we find the admonition "let your gentle spirit be known to all men." Why would Paul write this admonition to the true companion and not to the rest of the church? Wouldn't Paul want the entire church to demonstrate a gentle spirit? Didn't he know that Jesus said that it is the gentle that will inherit the Earth (see Matthew 5:5), and that gentleness is a fruit of the Spirit (Galatians 5:22-23)? Let's find out why.

First, we'll start with who the true companion is. When I investigated the specific identity of this individual, I have to be honest, I was disappointed. I couldn't find any definitive answers, and there were conflicting theories. Therefore, I decided to stick with what I firmly believe is true and rely solely on the Bible. When searching for clarification, I nearly always start with researching the words themselves, and I was relieved to find that I was no longer disappointed. I discovered that the Greek word used for this particular companion was *only* used in this passage. In other words, every single other time the word companion is written in the New Testament, a different Greek word was used. Now, what made *this* word different?

The word for companion in this verse is *suzugos* which means "yoke-fellow." It indicates a deep relationship that has a lot of history and, in that era, was often used to refer to one's spouse.[6] As a matter of fact, when I had researched theories as to who the true companion was, there are some who believe it was Paul's wife or lover.[4] In my opinion, however, there are two major flaws with that theory—the big one is found in the Bible itself where Paul talks about having the gift of celibacy. The other flaw is that Paul made his stance on homosexuality clear in 1 Corinthians 6:9-10 and Romans 1:26-27, and this word uses the masculine, not the feminine, ending.[4] But regardless of identity, this person was well-known and trusted by Paul and Timothy.

Now that we've established that this mysterious true companion had a deep fellowship with Paul, we are still left wondering why this person would be singled out from the rest of the church. My personal theory is that this individual had a leadership role in the church of Philipi. First, any responsible leader only allows trusted colleagues in charge in his/her absence, but mostly my opinion is based upon Philippians 4:2-3 where Paul says, "I urge Euodia and I urge Syntyche to live in harmony in the Lord. Indeed, true companion, I ask you to help these women who have shared my struggle in the cause of the gospel...." In this passage, we see that this person is specifically given instructions to engage in leadership activities, namely, resolving a conflict between two women. I have a hard time believing that Paul would allow an individual without leadership experience and authority to engage in such a challenging and delicate task. (On a side note, I love how Paul tells this person to engage in conflict resolution—everyone's favorite pastime—and then immediately tells him to "rejoice in the Lord always" in Verse 4. I don't know about you, but I don't think I'd be rejoicing over receiving or implementing those instructions.)

Paul is still talking to this true companion when he says, "Let your gentle (epieikés) spirit be known to all men," and we know this because he is still using grammatical markers in the singular form and hasn't shifted to address the brethren yet. As we saw when we began investigating this particular word translated as "gentle," this word literally means "on," "near," "over," and "fair/equitable" and, according to *Vine's Expository Dictionary*, this word is specifically used to convey interpersonal exchanges with others.[8,9] *HELPS Word-studies* offers further illumination by explaining that this word contains the notion of keeping the spirit of the Law and relaxing the strict standards of the letter of the Law. *HELPS* further explains that this concept builds upon (epi) what is really reasonable or reasonably intended by the Law. This makes it truly equitable (eikos). In my opinion, this facet of gentleness is best reserved for those in leadership, since it is our leaders who use written codes of conduct to make decisions that impact others, *especially* those decisions that are not clearly defined within that code.[2] (Though I have a sneaking suspicion that this true companion will be in need of this trait while resolving that conflict!)

One example that comes to my mind to illustrate this trait comes from my years as an undergraduate student. As part of my studies, I was required to take a statistics class. Math was never my strong suit, most likely because I found most of the higher-level math classes useless and all the practice required tedious. However, here I was in college and enduring another math class. As I was in agony while taking a test for this class, I came upon a question that I just *knew* I could answer if I could remember one step. Just one. That one step to a multi-step problem would unlock the entire problem, and yet there I was, stuck and racking my brain. I searched my memory and visualized my notes, my practice problems, and my textbook. But the elusive resolution was content to remain sequestered away in some hidden recess in the depths of my mind. I knew I needed every point I could get on this test, because the last thing I wanted to do was risk reliving the misery the next semester.

Finally, I decided enough was enough; I was just going to have to turn in the test as it was. My professor immediately noticed the empty problem and pointed it out, concerned that I had inadvertently skipped it. I hung my head in shame and confessed that I just couldn't remember how to do it. He paused, looked at me, and said, "How about I give you a hint in exchange for half the credit of the question?" I was shocked. No teacher or professor had ever offered that to me before. Yes! Oh, yes! Of course, I would take half-credit over no credit! He gave me the clue, I instantly remembered the necessary steps, took my test back to my seat, completed the problem, and received half-credit. That was epieikés in action. As the student, I had no right to request a hint for half-credit, but my professor decided to lax the strict code of test-taking (no help) for the spirit of the code (discerning whether or not the student retained enough material to solve the equation). Epieikés was a quality that engendered a wealth of gratitude from me on that day.

So, we see that epieikés is a valuable trait for a leader to show others. Imagine the impact of a leader who adheres only to the letter of the law, such as having a boss who insists you clock in at 8:00 every day, not 7:59 or 8:01. Solely adhering strictly to black and white policies can result in an extremely stressed out group of people. Now imagine a boss who expects you to be on time on a daily basis, with a reasonable window of grace, and is also understanding of life events such as traffic conditions, electricity going out overnight, and family emergencies. What a difference!

Finally, the third Greek word that is translated as "gentle" is épios. This word is not used as often as praüs and epieikés and is sometimes translated as "kind" instead of "gentle." This word appears twice in the New Testament and was often used by contemporary Greek writers to characterize authority figures who encounter challenging subordinates.[8] In the NAS version of the Bible, it appears as "gentle" in 1 Thessalonians 2:7, "but we proved to be gentle among you, as a nursing mother tenderly cares for her own children" and as "kind" in 2 Timothy 2:24, "the Lord's bond-servant must not be quarrelsome, but be kind to all." This word literally means "gentle," "placid," and "mild." According to *HELPS Word-studies*, this word also specifically refers to spoken words that are calming and bring God's order into a situation. *HELPS* further explains that it is through this mild demeanor that one is able to speak direct, straightforward, and honest truth into another's life while avoiding harshness.[3] What an incredible ability! If you're like me, you can recall more than one occasion when you stuck your foot in your mouth or said something that you immediately regretted. In all honesty, there are more instances than I care to remember over my lifetime that I wish I could go back and put some duct tape over my mouth. It would have caused less pain. I'm sure we've all experienced a lack of épios in our lifetime, whether on our part or someone else's, but what does it look like to experience épios?

I was lying in my bed, and my family was downstairs. Normally I take every opportunity to spend quality time with my husband and children, as our lives are hectic and family time is precious. However, I was going through a phase where it seemed as though nothing was going my way, I felt completely unappreciated by nearly everyone around me and, since I am a compulsive people-pleaser, I therefore felt I had nothing of value to offer. In other words, I was indulging myself in a royal self-pity party. As I listened to my kids having fun downstairs, I wallowed in mental slime.

Then I heard the footsteps. My husband entered our bedroom, sat on the bed, and looked at me. I half-heartedly glanced in his direction, and he proceeded to say, "Y'know, the kids and I really miss you downstairs." I shrugged him off. He lovingly put his hand on my shoulder and said something that shocked the truth right into me. He said, "You are wasting this beautiful day in this dark bedroom feeling sorry for yourself. Now, I love you, but the truth is, you're so focused on yourself, you're not even thinking about how this is impacting our daughters. The truth of the matter is, you're struggling with pride, and you will continue to be miserable as long as you allow pride to poison your mind and emotions."

His delivery was perfect. There was no hint of judgment in his voice, only love. There was no harshness, but rather an attempt to shine light into the darkness in my mind. And it worked. Those same words could have been spoken differently and could have caused a lot of damage to me and to our relationship, but the way he addressed me in that moment was pure épios. That épios created an instantaneous change in me as the revelation of his words pierced my soul. It took the chaos that I was allowing to control my mind and forced those twisted thoughts to align with God's order. His words were direct; they were straightforward and perhaps *slightly*, painfully honest. But they were spoken in love and spoken to bring peace to the turmoil within me. That's épios.

Let's just take a moment to compare the three Greek words we've discussed so far, since all three words demonstrate different angles of this characteristic. When differentiating between the words epieikés and praüs, *HELPS Word-studies* explains that praüs emphasizes the utilization of God's power under His control. According to *Vine's Expository Dictionary*, praüs also describes the disposition of a person.[8] Whereas praüs predominantly describes the nature of a person and how that nature impacts his/her actions, epieikés stresses active dealings with others.[2,5] In other words, praüs enables

7

us to impact others due to our willingness to allow God's power to work through us, and epieikés impacts others due to choices we make while associating with others. Epieikés does not emphasize a humble acceptance of God's will, it simply emphasizes actions taken while interacting with others.[9] Finally, while epieikés implies actions, épios implies words. Épios allows us to impact others specifically through speaking truth into someone else's life. This is a powerful trait, since sometimes truth can be difficult to deliver, and speaking God's truth in love has untold ability to make positive changes for someone else. Remember the parable of the sower from Matthew 13? The power of seeds of truth being sown in the fertile ground of someone's mind and heart can reap a harvest, maybe even a bumper crop.

Moving on to words translated as "gentleness," the first Greek word translated as "gentleness" in the New Testament is *praütes*, which is the noun version of praüs.[8] Nearly every occurrence of the word gentleness in the NAS version of the Bible is praütes. The exception is 1 Timothy 6:11, and the word used in that verse is praüs, which was already discussed.

In order to begin wrapping our minds around what this word means, try visualizing the most powerful force imaginable. Now magnify and intensify it. Now imagine harnessing that incredible power and using it to show grace and kindness. This condition perfectly describes the state of someone's heart and mind. This is praütes. Therefore, an individual is not gentle because they *lack* power; an individual is gentle because they *possess* power…immense power. An individual is gentle because they are able to take that power and wield it, and when they wield that immense power, they don't inflict harm but instead lavish kindness on the recipient.

To use a specific example, Isaiah 42:3 gives us a portrait of this characteristic when he writes, "A bruised reed He will not break, a dimly burning wick He will not extinguish." I've never handled a bruised reed, but I've burned my fair share of candles. As I'm sure many know, it is difficult to prevent a candle from going out when the wick is barely flickering. At that point, it doesn't need any help to snuff what remains of the flame; it self-extinguishes without a problem. In this passage God uses the imagery of a reed and a candle to teach His people because both items would have been common to the ancient Israelites. But what could these items represent? I believe they represent us, humanity.

Using the imagery of fire from this verse, we can liken His power to an erupting volcano or a sweeping forest fire. We are, of course, the flickering candle, barely able to garner the strength to emit an indistinct light in the shadows. Yet, when He reaches out to us and touches our lives, He doesn't stifle our flame. The grace, power, and kindness He possesses and embodies not only maintains our flame, it causes us to burn brighter and grow larger. Let me share a personal example.

I was in junior high, that lovely, awkward transitional phase where I developed from a girl into a young lady—and I was a mess. Depression and self-esteem issues cultivated a mental and emotional state that resulted in both an eating disorder and suicidal ideations. Looking back, it seems so hard to imagine that someone so young would consider life worthless and too difficult to continue, but there I was, struggling in silence day after day. No one knew how I *really* felt; a good Christian doesn't think these things, right? It would be years until I realized how my thoughts were wrong and misguided.

While no person knew the turmoil underneath the polished surface I presented, God certainly knew. Then one day, I had decided that this was it. It was the last day I was going to feel this way. I wrote a poem to say good-bye to my family and began to plan. As I contemplated which method would be the most effective with the least amount of discomfort, I felt God whispering in my heart. I tried to ignore Him, but He was persistent. Eventually, I began to listen—well, actually, to be more accurate, I began to argue.

After arguing (briefly, because, hey, who can really win a debate with God?) my reasons for wanting to end my life, God reminded me, gently and kindly, that my life didn't belong to me. He reminded me that He purchased my life on the cross and, therefore, I had no right to take what wasn't mine. Though those words may sound too harsh for someone who was in as fragile a state as I was at the time, they were perfect for me. And in that moment, He forever changed my mind, and my healing process began.

God, as our Creator, knows exactly what, when, and how to speak into our lives to bring that flicker to a blaze. God used His immeasurable power, delivered graciously and kindly, to reach into my soul at a time when my soul was imploding upon itself. His words and presence didn't break me. No, He didn't break me, rather He built me up. In that incredibly tenuous moment in my life, I needed a powerful word delivered with kindness and grace.

Honestly, I don't think a single good intention from any person would have been able to reach me as successfully, while also avoiding all harmful side effects due to the intensely negative state of mind I was in at this moment. God's perfect gentleness was just what I needed.

Ultimately, the incredible praütes gentleness of God enabled me to find peace and rest in my tumultuous soul. It was because of His gentleness that I was finally able to jettison the yoke that had been keeping me in bondage, preventing me from experiencing the freedom that Christ purchased for me. This moment with God and His gentle prodding in my heart and mind proved to be a fulcrum for change in my life. All was not perfect after this moment; it took years of prayer and some counseling, but I never hit such a low again. And the really cool ending to this story is that, right after I finished my (ahem) argument with God and turned the corner in my mind, two of my closest friends surprised me by pulling up in my driveway with a single red rose for me—just "because." Isn't God awesome?

Just as it was God's gentleness that was able to help me make a positive change in my life without causing damage to my unstable psyche, it is through gentleness that one individual is able to positively impact another without harmful side effects. Is it any wonder that God promises in Matthew 5:5 that people who demonstrate this characteristic will inherit the Earth? Living in such a way is bound to influence and inspire many, many people that we come into contact with.

Exploring Hebrew

Now that we've finished exploring the Greek words translated into English as "gentle" or "gentleness," it's time to continue the redefining process by taking a look at the Hebrew words.

The words "gentle" or "gentleness" do not appear very often in the Old Testament portion of the Bible. Actually, "gentle" only appears three times and "gentleness" once in the translation I use, the NAS. However, as I studied these four words, I was completely blown away, as what I discovered destroyed my previous beliefs regarding these words.

The first occurrence of the word "gentle" is in 1 Kings 19 and describes the way God spoke to Elijah after a great display of power in the natural world. In the original Hebrew, the word is *daq*. This word is used in other passages and is translated as "finely ground," "thin," "small," and "fine dust."[14]

God sets the stage for His gentle calling with a wind so powerful that it tore the mountain apart and shattered rocks. And that wasn't all! After that incredible wind, there was an earthquake. Think it's done? Think again. After the earthquake, there was a fire. Finally, after all that, came God's voice, gently blowing toward Elijah. Can you imagine the power of His gentle calling after such an immense display?

Take a moment to let that roll around in your mind and imagine standing on that mountain. Personally, I would have probably thought God's call came through His awesome display of power in the wind, the earthquake, and the fire. But Elijah proves to be more discerning than that. He knew that was merely a prelude to the real power—the presence of God Himself. He was able to discern that that show, while incredible, lacked the power of the quiet intimacy found in God's presence.

11

As I thought about what it would have been like to observe that display, I was struck by the genuine power that can be found in the quiet place. As I pondered this, a memory began to surface. I remembered volunteering at a vacation Bible school (VBS) in inner-city Philadelphia one summer. I was in my early teens, young, and inexperienced, and one of my jobs at this VBS was to help facilitate the lessons. This ranged from singing and dancing along to the songs to making sure the children were seated and quiet during the teaching.

Each day began with singing and dancing. Now, when there's a room completely filled with children, and they're singing, dancing, and being silly, do you think they just sit down "crisscross applesauce" nicely and quietly, fold their hands in their laps, and eagerly listen to the teacher? If you said, "Yes," and that was from personal experience, please pray for that same gifting in my life. As you can imagine, the host church's group of leaders had a difficult time corralling the children. The adults whistled, raised their voices in attempts to be heard above the ruckus, and clapped their hands, but it was mostly in vain. It took well over five precious minutes of time just to settle them enough to be heard above the din.

After getting the kids somewhat settled, the host church introduced our group, and one of the ladies from our group went to the front of the room in order to teach the lesson. She was a wonderful woman with a quiet demeanor who taught elementary students for a small Christian school in our area. I remember thinking she was toast. Maybe she could handle a classroom of kids with a church background from the country, but there was no way she would be able to handle this rowdy group. I couldn't have been more wrong.

In her quiet way, she sat down in the teacher's chair in the front of the room. But before she started her lesson, she took a moment to set one ground rule: whenever she raised her hand, the children were to raise their hand. When their hand was raised, they were not allowed to talk. I was dumbfounded at how effective this simple principle was. Those children were transformed into quiet, obedient, and attentive listeners. Sure, they acted up a little here and there, but up went her hand and, inevitably, so did theirs. The host church's group couldn't believe their eyes either. They had never seen them sit and listen so well. So, I guess it goes without saying that the host church's group immediately began implementing that same rule with the same result. No longer did they have to raise their voices to be heard above rowdy children, and there was no more whistling or hand-clapping. Just quiet. Quiet was more powerful than commotion. Just like in Elijah's story.

Seeing how powerful quiet is, is it any wonder that in Psalm 46 it says to "be still and know that I am God?" Many years ago, I wrote a song based upon this verse entitled "In the Stillness." Here are the lyrics to the final verse:

> In the stillness
> The silence speaks
> More powerfully than thunder
> Revelations of Your heart
> Proclamations of Your love
> Only in the stillness
> Can I know Your depths
> Can I feel Your heart beating
> It's only in the stillness

I have found the words of this verse and these song lyrics to be true time and again. When we quiet ourselves, we can hear the voice of God: that gentle voice that whispers in our minds and hearts and is so easily smothered by our thoughts and the busyness of life. Yet it's that gentle voice that also contains the power that created the stars and planets in the sky, breathed life into you and me, and shakes and crumbles every mountain in our lives—if we allow it to do so.

Quieting ourselves can be so hard in today's culture. Believe me, I know. Smartphones, computers, jobs, children, activities, and sports—so many things pull us in so many different directions. It can feel impossible at times to settle ourselves so we can listen for the Lord's voice but setting aside that time each day to quietly savor the presence of the Lord is crucial to living in the fullness of His presence and power in our lives.

The concept of quieting oneself has gained quite a bit of attention in the research world as, recently, researchers have been studying the impact of meditation. The results of these studies prove that setting aside time to meditate each day benefits both our minds and bodies. But before tuning me out and saying that meditation is not godly, recall that the Bible does say to "be still and know that I am God," and I can't think of any better description of meditating than quieting oneself and focusing on one or two thoughts, such as the awe of God or a Scripture verse. Furthermore, the word meditate is in the Bible seventeen times and meditation seven times. If doubts persist, take comfort in this: God commands His people to meditate on His law, and there are many examples of people in the Bible meditating on the wonder of God, His laws and statutes, and what He has done. So, now that biblical precedence has been established that it's okay to meditate within God-given parameters, let's take a quick look at what science has to say about the benefits of meditation.

For starters, meditation has been shown to decrease perception of stress.[10,21] This subjective finding has been corroborated by neuroimaging studies, as well as lab samples that measure levels of cortisol, the stress hormone.[10,22] Also, meditation has shown to improve overall mood, reduce depression and anger, and increase positive emotions.[13,21,23,27] Furthermore, it slows down our respiratory rate, which is associated with the parasympathetic nervous system.[2,6,9,26] Additional evidence for its association with the parasympathetic nervous system response can be found in meditation's beneficial impact on heart rate.[4,9,11,18,26] This is important because the parasympathetic nervous system has the opposite effect of the sympathetic nervous system.

But what does all of this mean? The sympathetic nervous system plays a very important role; it is responsible for preparing our bodies for intense physical activity, and is commonly known as the fight-or-flight response. This natural response is vital for emergency situations; however, its downside is that this system is also associated with stress and hypertension, quite possibly due to chronic, prolonged use by our bodies in situations that are not actual life-threatening emergencies.[4,5,21] When we activate the parasympathetic nervous system, though, it acts as the perfect antidote for this state of being by cancelling out that prolonged fight-or-flight response which is all-too-prevalent in our society.

Meditation also directly impacts the brain by promoting blood flow to that area of the body. This increased blood flow was found in multiple areas of the brain and included a part called the hippocampus which is responsible for helping to build new memories.[15,25] Interestingly enough, while meditation facilitated blood flow to the brain, it was also shown to lower blood pressure.[16]

Meditation's benefits continue beyond its impact on blood flow and blood pressure, as some studies show tentative evidence for positive effects on the immune system.[7,17] And, as if all these benefits weren't enough, meditation also improves our ability to empathize with others. One study even found that mothers who practiced mindfulness during pregnancy had children who exhibited less negative social-emotional behavior.[8,20] Is it any wonder why God would tell us to meditate? The God who knows every hair on our head and formed every part of our bodies knows the best way to maintain our physical and emotional health. Furthermore, the research cited in the above paragraphs used secular meditation techniques, now imagine what meditating on the Lord and His Word could do for our spiritual, physical, relational, and emotional well-being!

I know from personal experience the power of meditating on the Lord and Scripture. Growing up, I knew my mom meditated daily on Scripture verses, but I never bothered to learn much about it. She encouraged me to incorporate Scriptural meditation into my daily routine, but I always found something else to occupy my time. Until one summer I faced psychological challenges beyond what I had ever known, challenging enough to cause me to experience daily, uncontrollable panic attacks. In desperation, I reached out to a former college roommate who had recently completed her doctorate in neuropsychology. In addition to counseling, she advised me to begin to meditate. To Google I went.

I memorized the principles pretty quickly and began applying them that day. I started by meditating on 1 John 4:18, "perfect love casts out fear." Within two weeks, the uncontrollable panic attacks subsided and became manageable, and within two months all traces of those dreaded attacks were gone completely. What I found to be amazing was that all of these gains transpired while I was waiting to get in to the counselor's office. While I cannot promise the same impact for anyone else's life, as I can only share my own story, I can personally attest to the power of Scriptural meditation in my life and encourage others to make Scriptural meditation a regular part of their routine and see what God does!

The second time the word gentle appears in the Old Testament is in Proverbs. Here the Hebrew word is *rak* and means "tender," "delicate," and "soft." I hear it right now, "Wait a minute, Debbie, you said that gentleness was not synonymous with soft." And yes, according to the concordance the word stems from *rakak*, which means to be "tender," "weak," and "soft." From this root word, it might be tempting to say that our culture is right, that gentleness is the same as weakness. After all, even one of the words translated as "gentle" in the Bible came from a word that means to be weak. But before we bring the gavel down, let's look at this word in context.

This word, rak, appears in Proverbs 15:1 in the phrase "a gentle answer turns away wrath." We oftentimes associate anger with strength. We may feel strong when we are angry; any "weak" emotions like fear, shame, guilt, or sadness seem to dissipate in the presence of the awesome power of rage. To make it even more alluring, all we need to do is turn on any one of the many screens available to us to see this emotion in TV shows, movies, video games, and music. Anger and violence have become commonplace, and I would say even expected and glorified, in almost all of our media. Take a moment and reflect: how many times are the fights and arguments in our media won by the person who packs the biggest physical or verbal punch? And, furthermore, how many times is this portrayed as a positive rather than a negative?

There is, however, one secret weapon against anger—one weapon that, when wielded with wisdom and discernment, can overpower anger. Well, it isn't *that* much of a secret; it *is* in the Bible. Gentleness. Before we continue, though, please hear me out on one caveat: there are truly dangerous and abusive situations where an individual should, and must, remove himself/herself, and possibly others, for safety reasons. This verse should not be applied in those situations, and, in those cases, please seek safety and professional help. However, if that situation does not apply, gentleness can prove its power in relationships.

I'm sure we've all been there. Perhaps it was you, or a friend, a coworker, a client, a child, or a spouse. Yelling. Storming off. Slamming doors. Attempting to defy gravity with whatever happens to be the closest object. Let's just dig it up and get it out there. If you are a human being or live and associate with other human beings, the lost temper is bound to happen. We all get our buttons pushed at some point by someone. Just hopefully not in public.

Take a moment to think back over past arguments and fights. How do they usually go? Person "A" brings up a touchy subject, and maybe he/she was even nice, but Person "B" reacts negatively. This causes Person A to react negatively, and then Person B reacts even more negatively. And so on and so on and so on, until the two are in a screaming match. Is it possible to short-circuit what appears to be an inevitable cycle of ever-worsening anger and aggression? The Bible says, "Yes!" But only with a gentle answer.

Let's rewind the above scenario. Person A nicely brings up a touchy subject. Person B reacts negatively. Person A takes a deep breath, spends a few moments formulating a gentle, wise response, and Person B's aggression begins to melt away. After several exchanges where Person A continues to remain calm and gentle, Person B begins to mirror this response. In the end, the conflict is resolved peacefully. Sound like an impossible fairy tale? Let me share a few stories from my experience.

I work in a nursing home. As in any nursing home, we have patients with dementia, and these people can become aggressive. They are confused and, in that confusion, will often lash out at whoever is around. I cannot recount how many times I have been able to deescalate these patients simply by remaining calm. By maintaining open body postures (no crossed arms or legs, no hands on the hips), making no fast movements toward the person, having no tension in the face (and yes, sometimes I need to concentrate on it in the moment!), and by using a soothing tone, I have been able to calm a person who is hitting, kicking, chasing, throwing, and being verbally abusive. It does not usually happen after one exchange. It can take ten, fifteen minutes or more, and there is no guarantee the patient will respond positively. I have not been successful in every single attempt. That would be impossible. But I have been successful in many cases.

I remember one time in particular, when we had a very aggressive male patient. I was able to calm him down relatively quickly by using these techniques, but then someone else came down the hall and took a slightly aggressive tone with him. This person was not inappropriately aggressive, but the tone was just enough to destroy all the calming work I had done. The patient then regressed until he was just as agitated as he was when I had arrived. I started all over again and was successful again. Then this same person came back and undid the entire process again. Unfortunately, this semi-aggressive individual never took a cue and was not receptive to my explanations and advice, and around and around the aggression/calming cycle we went. However, each time the three of us cycled, I was awed by the consistent power of gentleness to diffuse the situation.

Think it only works with people who have dementia? Think again. Remember how I said we all get our buttons pushed? I have one child in particular who was blessed with the natural ability to push my buttons. All of them. I think she was particularly gifted from ages three to five. Unfortunately, during this time period, I had two other very small children and worked three jobs in my field. None of these jobs were full-time, but I was still overworked and under-rested. I'll spare you the painful details of all my personal failings. In the midst of this time, God, in His infinite grace and wisdom, in addition to the child who pushed all my buttons, also gifted me a child who knew how to "unpush" them. How did she do it? Let me share one story that is especially poignant in my memory.

We were in our dining room, and my buttons were getting pushed. Again. My challenging child was being defiant and was adopting an aggressive tone. I could just feel my blood pressure rising. The yell began to well up from my belly, through my boiling heart, into my throat, and as I struggled to maintain my composure, my lips snarled open. I didn't want to yell at her. Really, I didn't. I always felt like a failure when I succumbed to my temper, like I had failed as a human being and as a mother. I worried that I was a horrible example for my children, and I wanted better for them. With this in mind, I clenched my teeth and my fists, just hoping that would be enough to stave off the outburst that seemed inevitable.

In that instant, one of my other girls pulled on my sleeve. It jerked me out of the moment, but not completely. I had to remind myself not to explode on this innocent little girl because I didn't want collateral damage. I managed to look at her beautiful, angelic face and say, "What do you want?" in, admittedly, not the nicest of tones. She just looked up at me with her big eyes, blinked, smiled, and said, "I love you, Mommy."

Pssssssssssss. That's the sound of all that negative emotional pressure that had built up in me exiting my body. Instantly. And not because I exploded. Her beautiful, gentle words were just what I needed in that moment to safely release the tension from the boiling cauldron in my soul. I was then able to turn around and address my other child appropriately and resolve the situation in a constructive manner. It was incredible, and I can't tell you how many times this happened. Her amazing capability to intuitively understand that gentleness opposes anger wound up saving me from many lost tempers. Over time, it became easier and easier for me to make better choices on my own, but in the beginning, I needed help from someone else—even if that someone was under the age of five.

Just as my young daughter helped me find a better way, I have been able to share that gift with others in my house. For example, I have deescalated more than one argument with my husband through the wielding power of gentleness. It isn't easy, especially if I'm getting angered as well, but I have never regretted making the choice to take a deep breath, remain calm, and offer him a prepared response. I have, however, regretted NOT making that choice as the consequences negatively impacted our relationship and rippled throughout our family.

Notice two key words in that last paragraph. Choice and response. For me, remaining calm, thinking before I speak, and being aware of my facial expressions and body language is a choice I have to make each and every time. I am not blessed, as perhaps some are, in that this does not come naturally to me; my natural, human inclination is to react with anger when someone is dishing their anger out on me. However, I have come to realize that in every single interaction and situation we encounter in life, we have a choice: we can choose to respond positively, or we can default and react negatively. Default is easy. Choices can be hard.

Gentleness, after all, is a fruit of the Spirit. We have the choice to work together with God to grow this character in our lives, the choice to share this attribute with others, or the choice to leave it, undeveloped, on the proverbial tree in our souls. Making the choice to respond with kindness and gentleness is a powerful one, as the opposite, a default reaction tends to be associated with loss of control and power.

Taking steps to make the choice to grow in power by developing this attribute may not happen overnight, the next day, or even the next week. It takes time to mature, and it matures a little bit each and every time the decision is made to respond and not react. Speaking of decisions, have you decided which is more potent and a greater demonstration of power—gentleness or anger?

As we move on to the third time the word gentle appears in the Old Testament, we find ourselves in Jeremiah. In Verse 19 of Chapter 11, it says, "But I was like a gentle lamb, led to slaughter." Yes, yes, yes, again we have the association between the word gentle and lamb imagery, but let's take a closer look. When I initially began to research this term, which is *alluwph*, I thought I had found the one that would make my entire theory go kerflooey since in my concordance, the only definition given is tame, and this word is being associated with a lamb. But then I dug deeper.

As I delved into researching this term, I discovered that not only was this word translated as "gentle," but it was also translated elsewhere as "friend" and "chief." This is where it got really interesting. As I continued to research this term, I learned that the short definition is "captain." Captain? Lamb? Friend? Talk about confusing. I then looked to *Strong's Exhaustive Concordance* for answers and found that the word carries flavors of terms such as "guide" and "ox."[3] As I thought about all these complex nuances wrapped up within this one seemingly simple word, I reflected upon ancient Hebrew culture.

In ancient times, Hebrews used oxen to lead their plows. The oxen guided the plowman through the fields as they tilled, sowed, and harvested. Yes, there was a person controlling the oxen, but implicit within the concept of the ox is power and leadership; this concept was especially prevalent and important in ancient Hebrew culture. The ox may have been domesticated, tamed, and trained to drag a plow and a human being around a bunch of crops, but this did not negate the intrinsic raw strength within the animal. So, this begs the question: why would this term, alluwph, be juxtaposed with something as delicate as a lamb?

Unlike English, ancient Hebrew had more than one word for lamb; quite possibly because much of their culture centered upon agriculture, and shepherding in particular. In this verse, the word used for lamb specifically applied to sacrificial lambs. What could this mean? As I pondered the fact that this word, alluwph, a word that describes leadership and power, was being conjoined with a word that implies sacrifice, it all began to make sense. In this passage, we have an image of immense, inherent power, a power that is in submission, a power that is being used to lead and guide others, a power that is in a state of sacrifice. Jeremiah was using it to describe himself, but it also sounds an awful lot like someone else in the Bible. Now that doesn't sound like weakness or fragility to me.

Submission sounds easy until we have to do it. Self-control sounds easy until we have to do it. Sacrifice sounds easy until we have to do it. All of these things require great strength of character; they require the strength of an ox. Submission, self-control, sacrifice. All of these are traits that were exemplified by Jesus. All of these traits are ones He instructs us to implement in our lives. All of these traits are essential to excellent biblical leadership, and here in Jeremiah 11, we see these traits associated with being gentle.

The final Hebrew word associated with gentle in the Bible is found in Psalm 18. In this psalm, David writes in Verse 35, "Your gentleness makes me great." The word translated as "gentleness" in this verse is *anavah*, which more literally means "humility." Actually, the exact same prayer is recorded in 2 Samuel 22, but in 2 Samuel, there the word is translated as "help." Gentleness? Help? Humility? Could it be all three wrapped up into one? Perhaps it could be that the words in our language lack the depth and complexity found in the layered definition of Hebrew.

As I read and reread this verse, thinking about the significance of the word anavah, I began to realize that I didn't understand *how* it made David great. What did he mean by that? Back to the concordance I went, and there I discovered that in Hebrew, the words "make" and "great" in both passages were the same word! Now I was even more confused than when I started. Why would Hebrew use the same word twice, and why would we use two different words in English? According to ancient-hebrew.org, when a verb is repeated like this in a sentence, the purpose is for emphasis.[1] So, the next million-dollar question that I had was, what was so important that it had to be emphasized so emphatically?

The duplicated word is *rabah*. The simplest definition of rabah is "to multiply," and this word is used many times in the Old Testament for this simple definition.[19] However, as we just saw with the word gentleness, Hebrew words can carry a complexity of connotative and denotative meanings that are not completely translated in English. In other words, we lose some of the depth and tones found in the original language. As it turns out, this word does not *just* mean multiply. If it simply meant multiply, David could have been referring to his family (which was quite large) or his kingdom (which was ever-expanding under his rule). However, this word has a fuller, richer meaning than the simple mathematical mechanics of counting, adding, and multiplying, and I suspect David, a man after God's own heart, was using this word for exactly this purpose.

The word rabah contains the notion of the continual, ongoing process of growing up. In Ezekial 19:2 the word is translated as "reared" in the NAS and "nourished" in the King James Version.[24] I would venture to say that

David was crediting God with caring for him, parenting him, and helping him grow into maturity which, as any parent knows, is never-ending. It begins at conception and continues until death do us part. Parenting involves constantly investing in your children physically, emotionally, mentally, and spiritually. By using this verb twice, I believe David was emphasizing the fact that it was God who sustained him, God who taught him, and God who trained him to be the man he was.

Our New Testament doctrine may cause us to underappreciate what David wrote in this passage. In the days before Jesus, naming God as Father was unheard of and, quite frankly, impossible. However, in this prayer in Psalm 18, we get a glimpse of the incredibly intimate relationship that David shared with God. So intimate that, in a day and age where only ONE person could access God's presence behind a curtain ONCE a year, and ONLY after taking extreme care to follow every single mandated protocol down to each miniscule detail, David felt so close to God that he felt God had taken a parental role in his life. But how does this connect with gentleness?

Remember, it was God's gentleness/help/humility that sustained and matured David. Typically, it is the person who does the helping that has the greater strength and ability. The other person is dependent, unable to lift themselves out of their current situation. This is exactly how it is with us and God. In and of ourselves, we are unable to obtain salvation or develop sufficiently enough to accomplish His plan in our lives. However, through God reaching out and investing Himself in us, we are not only able to be saved and lifted out of our situations of complete helplessness, but we are also able to grow and achieve beyond what we could do or even imagine on our own.

Since this verb, rabah, connotatively involves the parent/child relationship, let's go back to this specific example. It is not the child who is able to mature himself/herself properly, and it is not the child who can sustain himself/herself. It is the parent, the older, more sacrificial, stronger and hopefully, wiser parent who guides and raises the child to maturity. This aspect of gentleness toward others has the power to touch them, sustain them, and help them develop into the people they were meant to be.

To sum up, the Hebrew words used for gentle or gentleness contain the flavors of control, submission, and sacrifice, and also seem to have a sense of tenderness, humility, stillness, and nurturing. However, also embedded within each of these words are the concepts of strength and power. The gentleness found in the Bible is able to conquer anger, promote connections within relationships, lead, and is even able to come alongside another person and help them overcome their challenges and develop them into maturity.

Down to the Letter

N ow that we've completed an overview of the Hebrew words that were translated as "gentle" or "gentleness," it's time to take a closer look at these words by dissecting them letter by letter, as we continue to redefine this amazing attribute. I've chosen to examine the Hebrew words in this way since Hebrew is the original language of God's chosen people, and each letter of the Hebrew alphabet represents specific concepts. As I conducted research, I felt that exploring these concepts and how they relate to each other provided greater insight into the biblical definition of gentle and gentleness.

As a speech-language pathologist, linguistics was part of my coursework. During these classes, I became intrigued with the roots of our language. After graduating, I continued to read literature about the history of the English language and the alphabet. By doing this, I discovered that the English and Hebrew alphabets have a common ancestry. While researching for this book, I decided to put this potentially trivial interest to good use and wound up unearthing some gems. In this section, I'll provide a brief history behind the letters, and then a synthesis and analysis of the possible significance of the combination of the concepts represented by those letters as it relates to gentleness.

We'll begin by investigating the Hebrew letters used in the first word translated as "gentle" in the Old Testament, daq (remember the story of Elijah and God's gentleness after the wind, fire, and earthquake?). The Hebrew letters used to write this word are *qoph* and *dalet*, and since Hebrew was read right to left, we'll start with dalet, the predecessor to our letter *D*.[13,14,15] Originally dalet simply meant "door" and "opening" but, over time, its definition evolved, and dalet also came to contain many other concepts including "circulation," "resulting from," "abundance," "to disseminate," "to pour," "bucket," "humility," "enter," and "leave."[13,16]

The other Hebrew letter used in daq is qoph. Qoph was taken from the 19th letter of the Phoenician alphabet, shares the same place in the Hebrew alphabet, and is the predecessor to our own Q.[16] Outside of that bit of history, though, scholars begin to disagree and multiple opinions surface.

There are several theories as to what qoph originally meant, and I will share the dominant theories here. Perhaps only one is true, or perhaps all of them are, but one popular theory is that qoph meant "monkey" or "ape" while other popular theories are that this letter meant "eye of the needle" or "a hatchet/cleaver/ax."[13,16] One scholar also wrote that this letter grew over time to convey the concepts of transmitting life, "excavating the depths," and "a moment separated from the flow of time."[16] When looking at Hebrew words that begin with this letter, however, many of them share the concept of cutting, separation, or interruption.[13]

As I pondered the juxtaposition of these concepts—a separation or dissemination of life followed by an open door—I was struck by the fact that in the story of 1 Kings 19, it was within the presence of God that these ideas were found. It is within the presence of God that we are sanctified (set apart or separated from the world), it is the presence of God that opens the door for us to have a new and abundant life, and it is He that pours His life into ours so we can share it with others. Furthermore, recall that in this story, it was God's presence that manifested quietly despite the wholly tumultuous surroundings that Elijah found himself in. God's presence is the peace in our storms; it is a constant source of rest and quiet. In order for us to experience the quiet rest in His presence, however, we need to quiet our flesh and lean into Him. It is often in the quiet place that we are able to allow the depths of our being to search and find the depths of His. It is through this intimacy that we are able to walk in God's blessing and fulfill the plans that He has for us. This begins when we put an end to our fruitless efforts at righteousness and find rest in His free gift of salvation through His Son. This is how we walk through the door and enter into relationship with God; by continuing to rest our souls in His presence, we are continually sanctified and empowered through His Spirit. To put it in other words, we are able to walk through the doors that He opens for us when we separate ourselves from the desires of this world and allow our souls to rest in Him.

Therefore, the concept of separation providing open doors and new life is central to Christianity. It was only by separation that the doors to intimacy with our Lord can be established. Humanity had to be separated from sin in order to open the door to relationship with God. However, for this to happen God had to separate Himself from Jesus when He took that burden on the cross. Remember what Jesus said on the cross, "My God, my God, why have You forsaken me?" Many believe it was in this moment that the sin of humanity was placed upon Jesus and, since God in His holiness cannot coexist with sin, He had to separate Himself from Jesus when this happened. However, it was through this ultimate separation that ultimate intimacy was achieved. God gave us proof of this new intimacy when He tore the veil to the Holy of Holies in two from top to bottom as Jesus breathed His last breath. If this sacrificial exchange of Jesus's life for ours had not happened, we would have continued in sin, hopelessly and endlessly, and would never know the quiet rest that is found in His presence. So, in God separation (qoph) opens the door to new, abundant life (dalet).

The second Hebrew word for gentle is rak. Rak is comprised of two Hebrew letters, *kaph* and *resh*. Again, following in the Hebrew tradition of reading right to left, we'll begin analyzing this word's Hebrew letters with resh. This letter has a long history, as it was found amongst the oldest alphabetic writings which were discovered in archaeological digs in central Egypt.[16] This letter then made its way to Phoenicia as the 20th letter of their alphabet and, from there, it found its way to the Hebrew alphabet and finally made it into our alphabet as *R*.[15] Originally, this letter looked like the profile of a human head and meant "head" or "beginning."[13, 16] While resh continued to literally mean "head" or "beginning," it later derived several additional meanings including "create," "creation," "brain," "cranium," and "priority," and in Hebrew culture this letter wound up adopting an interesting connotation of extremes.[13] I did not find any definitive evidence as to why this is the case, but perhaps it was because the head was at the absolute top of our bodies. However, there are instances in Hebrew writing where the use of this letter conveyed the idea of extreme opposites such as "top and bottom," "rich and poor," and "first and last."[13]

The second letter used to spell rak is kaph, from which we get our own letter *K*. Kaph was the 11th letter of the Phoenician and proto-Sinaitic alphabet and, originally, this letter stemmed from an ancient Egyptian hieroglyph that showed a side view of a hand. The early Semites put their own twist on this original pictogram and used a picture of an upright hand.[16] The name, kaph, literally meant "palm of hand" as well as "to take" and "to give." Over time, kaph also came to encompass the concepts of "trade," "to bless," and "to cover."[13]

In ancient Hebrew, not only were words read from right to left, but adjectives also came after nouns.[14] Therefore, when the Jews read the word rak, they first read the symbol for head and then read the symbol for hand. I'll take the liberty of utilizing the grammatical rule of noun then description, and using this pattern of construction, the symbol for hand modifies the symbol for head. Therefore, we have a head being described as giving or taking, being covered, or blessed.

The notion of hands being used to transfer blessing is exemplified in the Old Testament of the Bible through stories such as Jacob blessing his grandsons, Ephraim and Manasseh. Additionally, David alluded to God's blessing and protection in our lives as a result of God's hands covering us when he wrote in Psalm 139, "You have enclosed me behind and before, and laid Your hand upon me. Such knowledge is too wonderful for me, it is too high, I cannot attain it." Other symbolic actions the ancient Jews associated with the hands were transferring the sin of the people to animals during sacrifices and transference of authority, such as when Moses passed the proverbial baton to Joshua.

In addition to discussing the possibility that this pair of symbols is significant for transferring blessing or representing protection, though, I would be remiss if I didn't also discuss the importance of head coverings in Jewish culture in general. The tradition of covering one's head was established centuries ago and continues to this day. Men typically wear a small skullcap called a yarmulke, or sometimes called a kippah, and women oftentimes completely cover their heads with a veil or scarf although, recently, in some places, women have taken to wearing fashionable hats instead.[3,9] Traditionally, only married women covered their heads, and they did so as a sign of modesty.[3,9] Regarding the men, however, originally only priests and scholars covered their heads as a sign of their position in society but beyond these men, only mourners and lepers wore a head covering.[9] However, over time, more and more men began to adopt a head covering. Though initially they only covered their heads during prayer, at meals, and when studying sacred writings, as the centuries passed, men began to wear a covering all the time.[3]

Why? Why would a culture go from only select men wearing a head covering to all men wearing a covering? Why would this culture go from only wearing a covering sometimes to wearing a covering at all times? The answer is simple: this covering gained religious significance within their culture. Rather than simply denoting societal hierarchies or certain conditions, the covering came be a physical representation of their reverence for God and of their relationship with God.[3,9] Therefore, this pair of symbols can also signify both respect for God and relationship with God.

As I considered these Hebrew letters, resh and kaph, within the context of ancient Jewish culture and Proverbs 15:1, "a gentle answer turns away wrath," I began to realize that, perhaps, there was an implication that went deeper than the definition found in my concordance. The denotative definition found in my concordance was "tender," "delicate," and "soft." However, the context of the verse, coupled with the letters used to portray this concept, indicates a power much greater than what any dictionary could describe.

First, I found it intriguing that in the NAS version of the Bible, this is the only verse that uses rak to convey the concept of gentle. For one, let's consider the implied setting of this verse—a conflict or, at the very least, one person is upset with another. In this context, it is rak that turns away wrath. Rak, the word that contains the Hebrew letter for head. It is within our heads that our thoughts are conceived and percolate. It is our minds that breed thoughts of anger, jealousy, grace, and joy. It is rak that has the power to divert the negative emotions of anger and wrath, and it does this through responding with blessing and tenderness. In this verse, rak is being paired with "answer" (also translated as "response" elsewhere), and this indicates that a responsive action is required.[12] A response, not a reaction. A response requires thought and planning and goes beyond a knee-jerk. A response uses the mind. It is this response of blessing that, when implemented correctly, has the power to divert anger.

Not only do the letters of rak contain the notion of a response of tenderness and blessing, but they signify protection as well. It is my experience and observation that walking through life with an inclination to bless others offers protection for our own minds. In my experience, whenever I become focused on myself, my thoughts, and therefore attitudes and behavior, go down the toilet (remember my royal self-pity party...case in point!). However, God, in His grace, time after time, opens my eyes so I can see my self-destructive ways and put my focus back where it belongs— on Him and others. Also, to be honest, I've never met a happy selfish person; every single one of them thinks that focusing on their own lives, perceived needs, and desires will make them happy. Unfortunately, that kind of thinking it is just a deception that leads to a twisting descent. Each one that I have met is miserable and irritable which, of course, makes them more prone to respond in anger when someone is upset with them. This is because living a selfish life perpetuates misery and destructive attitudes. But living a life of selflessness and blessing, from my experience, promotes positive attitudes and resilience.

Not only does living a life of blessing to others protect our own minds, it can offer protection for another person's mind as well. This will be discussed more in Chapter 6, but to briefly summarize, self-righteous, self-serving anger, just like any other type of selfishness, is another seductive path that sends us spiraling downhill in a hurry.[4, 5, 6, 8] Also, anger is highly contagious and, therefore, anger feeds on and generates more anger.[2,11] What better way to protect everyone's minds than to break the cycle? Rak enables us to do just that.

Not only do the letters that comprise rak provide insight into the protective power of living a life of blessing and tenderness toward others, they also reveal how to live this lifestyle: through a relationship with God. God's love and presence in our lives protects our minds. There are three instances in the Bible where God describes salvation as being a helmet: Isaiah 59, Ephesians 6, and 1 Thessalonians 5. What better protection for our heads than a helmet? From children on bicycles to our military, helmets are the go-to for protection for one of our most valuable pieces of anatomy. And what offers protection to our spiritual heads? God's salvation—a relationship with Him.

It is through our relationship with Him that we are able to respond with blessing in the face of anger and even persecution. When we actively engage with Him and allow His thoughts to shape ours, we utilize His protective helmet of salvation, and this means that the assaults of wrath just deflect right off of our minds. His love in our lives not only helps us to respond with blessing when someone is unleashing anger our way, it also helps us to stand victorious in the midst of it. Rak protects our minds (resh) and the minds of others, because God's presence in our lives enables us to respond with tender blessings (kaph) and endure the flaming darts of selfishness hurled at us by those who care only for themselves.

The third Hebrew word translated as "gentle" is alluwph, which literally means "captain." This Hebrew word is used sixty-nine times in the Old Testament, is only translated as "gentle" once, and uses four Hebrew letters: "pe," "vav," "lamed," and "aleph." When reading this word, aleph would have been the first letter read by the Jews. Aleph was the first letter of their alphabet and has maintained its position as the first letter of our alphabet through our letter *A*.[15] The word aleph meant "ox," and this letter was originally a pictorial representation of an ox head.[16]

Why an ox? As already discussed, the ancient Jews had a very agrarian society; they lived on the land, and their lives were centered on farming. The ox was most likely the strongest animal available with which to plow and harvest. The fortitude of the ox was therefore incredibly valuable to their culture for, without it, the ancient Jews would have had a much greater challenge in their quest for survival. Because of this importance, the ox came to represent a powerful and indispensable force that set everything for life into motion; it came to be revered as necessary for life.[13] Therefore, this letter, aleph, came to symbolize possibility, beginning, strength, and being, and in Jewish culture also came to represent champion, prince, and to teach.[13]

The next letter is lamed. Lamed was the 12th letter of the proto-Sinaitic alphabet and is the precursor to our 12th letter, *L*.[15] Originally this letter took the form of an ox goad which was a stick used to coax cattle into moving; in other words, to prod the animals along to get them to do their jobs.[15] Originally, this letter symbolized the concept of causing motion, to change from a restful state to a state of action, and to promote.[13] However, over time, this letter acquired many additional derivative meanings including "to learn," "study," "to teach," and "expand."[13] It is unclear exactly how these derivative meanings developed, but perhaps they evolved from the concept that the cattle learn where to go and how to behave through the goading and prodding of their caretakers. After all, no one learns by doing nothing; it is only through taking action that we learn. We learn from achieving, we learn from mistakes, we learn through correction, but we don't learn when we sit around and do nothing.

The third letter is vav, which is also referred to as *waw* by some scholars. Vav was the 6th letter of the proto-Sinaitic alphabet, and this single letter spawned not one, not two, but four of our English letters. *F, U, V,* and *W* can all thank vav for their existence.[7] The meaning of this letter is almost as variable as the quantity of letters it engendered.

In the proto-Sinaitic alphabet, vav was an oar and carried with it the concept that it linked one place to another by providing safe transport by boat.[13] In the Phoenician alphabet, the word waw meant "peg" and the letter was shaped somewhat like a capital Y, and in Hebrew, the word vav meant "nail."[13,16] Despite the variability in the original meanings of this letter, they all share one concept: connection. This connotation permeates this letter, and the letter itself can be used as a conjunction in Hebrew grammar.[14] When it used as a conjunction, it is equivalent to "and" in English where it acts to add, specify, or complete meanings.[14]

The 4th, and final, letter of alluwph is pe, the predecessor to our letter *P* and also the 17th letter of the Phoenician alphabet.[15] The name of this letter meant "mouth," and the shape originally looked somewhat like a smiling mouth.[16] Since the mouth is associated with eating, speaking, and breathing, all of these concepts are contained within this letter.[13] Hebrew culture has cultivated additional meanings, specifically, memories or history that are passed orally as well as the oral law.[13]

In the Bible, God admonishes the Israelites on more than one occasion to *tell* their children about Him, His works, and His law, giving "pe" more than just a little significance in Hebrew culture. After Israel's exodus from Egypt, God gave His nation His law and with it, an explicit command to make His commandments known to their children. This account is found in Deuteronomy 4:9-11, and a couple of chapters later in Deuteronomy 6:6-7, God tells the Israelites to make sure that:

> *These words, which I am commanding you today, shall be on your heart. You shall teach them diligently to your sons and shall talk of them when you sit in your house and when you walk by the way and when you lie down and when you rise up.*

Jewish culture reveres God's law, and for centuries the Jews adhered to both a written law, the Torah, and an oral law. The oral law was highly revered in Jewish culture. The rabbis, or the culture's religious leaders, believed that the oral law stemmed from the time of Moses, and they saw it as a legitimate supplement to the written law. So, the oral law was considered as equally valuable and contained an equal amount of authority as the written law and, together, the oral and written laws were considered the core of Jewish religion and culture.[10]

However, the oral law was not the only oral tradition of great importance to the ancient Jews; oral history was highly valued as well. In a day and age when people wrote with chisels or styluses on clay, stone, wood, wax, or shards of broken pottery, oral communication was key to keeping family history and traditions alive.[17] So, one can imagine that oral history traditions were considered the gold standard and received greater emphasis in this ancient culture since they were less expensive, more portable, and weren't considered vulnerable to decay or loss.[3,17] Any written accounts of Israel's history were often in the form of a scroll which was stored away; hard copies merely served as a backup for the ancient Israelites.[17]

Oral communication was, therefore, of utmost importance to the ancient Jews, which brought a great deal of importance to the letter pe. In my humble opinion, pe embodies what was essential for Jewish life to endure—eating and breathing for their physical survival as well as oral communication for building relationships and to ensure that their culture and faith continue through the generations.

How do these four letters provide further enlightenment regarding the concept of gentleness? First of all, let's take a moment to refresh our minds regarding the context for this particular word. Jeremiah was referring to himself in Chapter 11 and Verse 19 when he says, "But I was like a gentle lamb led to the slaughter." Remember that the word for lamb was specific to a sacrificial lamb, and that the word gentle had nuances of friend, guide, and captain? Good—let's dive in.

We begin with the concept of the ox, this beast symbolizing teaching, leadership, life, possibility, and power. Next, we come to the ox goad, which signifies a catalyst for change, movement, learning, and study. Third, we have a symbol of connection, intimacy, addition, and completion. And finally, we have a representation of speaking, sharing memories and history, and breathing. But how do these concepts blend together to form one concept—the concept of gentle?

First, this word, alluwph, begins with immense power and potential (aleph) which is mobilized and controlled (lamed). This controlled power is focused toward another, and an intimate bond is forged (vav). Next, this connection results in growth and maturation which eventually results in sharing with others, and additional discipleship occurs (pe). Inevitably, as this process continues, more and more lives are impacted. As I researched the concepts involved in this specific word, I was struck by the incredible foreshadowing technique that God used here. I really shouldn't have been surprised, though; after all, God is the master of detail and complexity and knows the end from the beginning, but my limited human abilities had me staggering, in awe of God's masterful craftsmanship.

Remember that the word alluwph in this verse was specifically being applied to a sacrificial lamb. It would be many years before the final sacrificial Lamb was to appear; yet here we have a glimpse into God's promise and plan in the book of Jeremiah, all wrapped up in a singular word. Let's break down this foreshadowing letter by letter. What greater power is there than God (aleph)? God set aside His glory and took on human flesh, as Jesus Christ, which was the mobilization of His power toward us (lamed). Then through His controlled power, He made a way to forge an intimate bond with humanity through the death and resurrection of His Son, which brought new life, completion, and spiritual growth to us (vav). And finally, after God places His love and life in our hearts, we share this new love and life with others (pe), and the process of discipleship and growth begins all over again. In the words of my daughter, that's incredimazing!

It's time to move onto the 4th, and final, Hebrew word used to convey the attribute of gentleness in the Old Testament, which is anavah. This particular word is used only six times in the Old Testament and, of those six occurrences, only two were translated into English as "gentleness." Anavah literally translated means "humility," and to spell this word, the Jews used four letters: *ayin, nun, vav,* and *he.*

Ayin originated in ancient Egypt as a hieroglyph that depicted a human eye.[15] Its position moved from the 16th letter in the proto-Sinaitic alphabet up to the 15th letter of ours, where it eventually became our letter *O,* however, it was originally a consonant.[7,13] Ayin contains the obvious association with the eye and vision, but over the years has derived many additional concepts. Continuing with the vision and eye theme, ayin has also come to mean "appear/disappear," "visible/invisible," "obscure," "opaque," and "to gaze."[13] In the Hebrew culture, ayin also indicates a spring or source of water.[13] Since springs have moving water, this letter also came to imply movement, specifically from the inside to the outside and from the concealed depths of the Earth to the surface. Since springs flow from underneath the surface of the Earth, ayin can also mean "revelation with concealment."[13]

The second letter used in anavah is nun. Since nun is the predecessor to our letter N, it appears as though it has remained comfortable in the 14th slot of both the proto-Sinaitic and English alphabets.[16] The name nun came from the Phoenicians and meant "fish" however, the shape itself was the result of an Egyptian hieroglyph that depicted a snake.[15] As with the other letters already covered, this letter also evolved and acquired additional meanings over time. Quite possibly because fish are in water, and water tends to conceal and be mysterious, nun also came to mean "hidden," specifically "hidden depths that are not visible."[13] This letter also grew to mean "forthcoming birth and life," possibly because an unborn child is concealed in fluid within the mother's womb.[13]

The 3rd letter is vav which was already covered in the discussion of alluwph. As a brief reminder, this letter denotes connection, addition, and completion.

The final letter used to create this word is "he" which was the 5th letter of the proto-Sinaitic alphabet and is the precursor to our 5th letter, E.[16] The original shape of this letter was a half-crouched human stick figure with arms bent at the elbows in a raised position, possibly toward heaven.[16] If you flip our letter E on its side, with the long, singular straight line on the ground, you can almost visualize the two uplifted arms and a head in the middle.

The original meaning of this pictograph in ancient Semitic culture was "prayer," and the name he most likely originally meant "the sound of breathing."[13] The significance of these meanings have lived on in Jewish culture, as the meaning of he has grown to include "soul," and "life," since it is with our first breath after birth that we begin our life in this world, and thanks in part to repeated, daily respirations that we are able to continue our existence.[13] However, the initial denotative meaning of this letter was prayer. Prayer is central to Jewish culture, and there are some in Jewish culture that say that the sound of breathing is the original sound of prayer.[13] Thus, it is clear that the symbol, he, depicted someone praying, and one could argue that all life, both physical and spiritual, are given and perpetuated by God. To be more specific, since prayer is one of our primary connections to God, then prayer is, like breathing, a part of what sustains and renews our lives. Finally, as an end note, this letter is often used at the end of Hebrew words to indicate movement toward whatever came before it.[14] Just as God came before us and initiated connection with us through His call and through Jesus's sacrifice, prayer moves us toward Him. As we maintain a lifestyle of prayer, we continually grow closer to Him and deepen our relationship with Him. It is through this movement, enabled by prayer, that we are then able to move powerfully into what He has planned for our lives. Prayer enables us to move toward God and our destiny.

Once again, there are four concepts merging together in this word, anavah, to create a singular concept called gentleness. First, this word begins with vision, concealed revelation, and a spring which is followed by a fish, hidden depths, and forthcoming birth. Subsequent to this are connection, intimacy, completion, and addition and, finally, this concept ends with prayer, breathing, life and movement toward the preceding concepts.

Before discussing the analysis of this conglomeration of concepts, however, let's take a quick peek at the verse in which this word is used. This particular word, anavah, was translated as "gentleness" in Psalm 18:35, "Your gentleness makes me great." As discussed in Chapter 2, this verse specifically speaks of nurturing, sustaining, and helping someone become who they were meant to be.

When investing in someone's life, whether it is a child within our homes or someone we are choosing to mentor spiritually, it is important to begin with a vision of what could be. For example, as a mother, I teach, guide, and discipline my children because I have a vision of what type of adult I hope they become. This is my vision and, ideally, a godly vision for their lives. It is a concealed revelation because, short of a prophetic word from the Lord, I cannot foresee their futures. Therefore, my hopes and vision for the lives of my children are like looking through murky waters: I have a general idea but no specifics. Despite this poor view into their future, adult lives, I sacrificially pour my heart and soul into them while holding to the belief that they will grow into adults that accomplish the plans that God has for them.

It is this investment on my part that is the catalyst for engendering new thought and behavior patterns within my children. These new thoughts and behaviors usually begin small, sometimes so small I can't perceive them but, nevertheless, the seed (the nun) is planted. The seed begins a new way of life within each child's mind and heart and then grows and matures within them until the resulting fruit is clearly evident to all. This is not a quick process. In fact, it can take a lifetime; for just as physical development from conception to birth takes time, so does mental, emotional, and spiritual development. This maturation process takes patience and love (vav).

It is only through consistent, loving, sacrificial investment that the vision (ayin) that planted the seed (nun) is able to flourish. Continuing with the example of the parent/child relationship, what would happen if I, as a mother, only provided instruction to my child once? No follow up. No discipline. No guidance. Just a word in passing. I guarantee that if this is how I parented, my children would learn nothing, and they would gain nothing. When I began the journey of parenthood, I learned very quickly that parenting boils down to patience and perseverance. Why else would the Bible admonish parents to teach their children from the rising to the setting of the sun? God knows that loving, consistent guidance from someone that we are deeply connected to is the most effective way to create a lasting impact. That kind of patient, perseverant, and sacrificial investment is the best way to cultivate hearts and produce the fertile environment needed to generate positive rewards that can be reaped by all.

The final letter, he, expresses the idea of prayer, life, and movement toward because in order for the above-mentioned process of investing and nurturing to be successful, it requires prayer. Prayer, or personal communication and fellowship with God, is what brings renewed strength on those days when we just can't give any more. When we can feel ourselves snapping inside, prayer can breathe the life of God into our souls. Prayer is like taking a deep spiritual breath…a few deep natural breaths from time to time don't hurt either.

As mentioned in the previous paragraph, this letter also conveys the idea of movement toward. Therefore, it is the act of moving toward the vision that plants the seed that creates new life and intimate connection, which then helps the person be who they were meant to be. It requires action. Not just thoughts: action. Not just words: action. We need to be actively planting seeds of love and seeds of vision while continually, actively moving toward that connection, growth, addition, completion, and vision. That is true discipleship. It's not a one-day thing; it's a long-haul thing, and maybe even a lifelong thing. And what better way to move toward new growth and vision than prayer?

Discipling another person may seem overwhelming, but the rewards reaped from living this lifestyle should not be underestimated. In my opinion, there is no greater privilege or satisfaction than to pour myself into someone else and, with God's blessing and favor, see real change and growth over time. Furthermore, according to Matthew 28:19-20, discipling others is a direct command from Jesus, which means that we are all called to disciple others during our time here on Earth.

As I close this portion of the book, I wanted to take a moment to point out something that I found pretty amazing. I was struck by some of the similarities between the four Hebrew words used to convey the concepts of gentle/gentleness and the Greek words. The essence of the four Hebrew words is: responses of tender blessings; humility, nurturing; power in stillness and the quiet place; and a friend who leads or guides. The core principles of the Greek words are spoken words that bring God's order without harshness; being fair, just and adhering to the spirit, not the letter of the law; and great power wielded with self-control to show kindness and grace to others. All of these words share qualities of power, leadership, self-control, kindness, humility, grace, and connection and challenge us at both the individual and the interpersonal levels. Regarding the individual level, they confront the thoughts and attitudes we choose. When it comes to relationships, all these words deal with our verbal and nonverbal communication, our actions toward others, and finally these words address how leaders should be conducting themselves while operating in a position of authority. I have one, final question before we explore the key attributes of gentleness and how modern research confirms the truth of God's principles: have you decided which one is a better representation of gentleness—a lamb that plays and follows its mother around, or a lioness that controls her power to rear her cubs?

Digging Deeper

Power

Royalty. Presidents. CEOs. What do these positions have in common? Power. According to *Merriam-Webster's Dictionary*, power is "the ability to produce an effect; possession of control, authority, or influence over others; physical might."[26] Since we have already established that the attribute of gentleness contains power, this chapter will investigate two types of power: God's power in our lives and natural power. For some, these concepts may take time to acquire and be might uncomfortable initially; however, through practice and application, a wallflower can become the centerpiece of a bouquet.

The first type of power covered in this chapter in a Christian's life isn't ours. While it takes one decision and one millisecond for us to possess it, we don't own it, and we can't get any more of it. There's nothing we can do to make it greater, but we can choose whether or not we're going to allow it to work in us and through us and to what capacity. This power is God's.

Did anyone hear that thud? That's the sound of me hitting the ground in shock. It never ceases to amaze me that the God who created the universe actually resides in me. *In me!* This immeasurable, unlimited power fits in the confines of my mortal body. Somehow. I can't explain exactly how it works, so I suppose it's one of those realities that will remain a mystery to me until I enter heaven. That being said, the Bible does talk quite a bit about God's power in our lives.

The topic of God's power is *huge* and will not fit within the confines of this chapter. For example, in the NAS version of the Bible the word translated as "power" has twenty-two different original Greek and Hebrew words. Twenty-two! A topic this grandiose could easily fill volumes, but I will attempt to provide a brief overview here. Before I continue, please understand—I'm not a fan of following formulas to extract what you want from God, in this case power, so I won't say this is a formula. But I *will* say that, in my opinion, there are spiritual principles, and I believe that living our lives in such a way that they enable God's power to move in us and through us falls into this category. If I were to create a diagram to illustrate this spiritual principle, it would look like this:

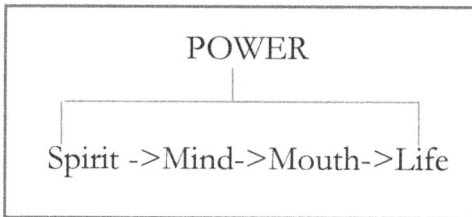

```
┌──────────────────────────────────────────┐
│                                            │
│               POWER                        │
│                 │                          │
│        ┌────────┴────────┐                │
│        │                 │                 │
│   Spirit ->Mind->Mouth->Life              │
│                                            │
└──────────────────────────────────────────┘
```

Let's dissect this diagram piece by piece.

Allowing God's power to work through our lives begins in the spiritual realm. As long as we have truly accepted Jesus as our Lord and Savior, we *already have all* of God's power within us. Any doubts? Paul provides an excellent reminder of the reality of God's power in our lives in Romans 8:9-17 when he says:

> *You have not received a spirit of slavery leading to fear again, but you have received a spirit of adoption as sons...the Spirit Himself testifies with our spirit that we are children of God, and if children, heirs also, heirs of God and fellow heirs with Christ.*

In other words, since spiritually we are God's children, we have every single resource available to us that Jesus walked in when He was on Earth. Was Jesus able to withstand temptation through God's power? So can we. Was Jesus able to perform miracles? We can too. We, through obedience to the Lord, are able to allow His power to perform incredible, supernatural, miraculous acts through us. Furthermore, according to this passage, the *Spirit Himself* says this is true. Therefore, this isn't just Paul spouting off empty promises; these verses make it sparklingly clear that the Holy Spirit Himself has declared this to be true.

God's power lives in us! His power, that broke our spiritual bondage to sin according to Romans 8:9 ("you are not in the flesh but in the Spirit") and raised *"Christ Jesus from the dead"* (emphasis mine) according Verse 11 lives in each and every believer. This means that within the spirit of every born-again follower of Jesus is the power to live in complete spiritual freedom and abundant life. But how does this happen?

The moment Christ enters our hearts we are set free from spiritual death and bondage. Free from the power and control of sin. Free to experience God's life. Free to walk in the power of God. FREE! And it gets even better! Romans 6:5 says, "For if we have been united Him in the likeness of His death, certainly we will also be in the likeness of His resurrection." In other words, not only do we have freedom and life in Christ, we are actually spiritually united with Him. It is this spiritual unity with God that enables us to possess His power and is the source of our *experience* of His power *in* our lives and the *manifestation* of His power *through* our lives.

Through Jesus's sacrifice, we are given unity with God. Yes, *given*. No longer do we need to perform the bloody ritualistic sacrifices described in the Levitical Law for an occasional fleeting taste of God's presence; Jesus was our perfect sacrifice and gave us complete, daily access to the Lord. Furthermore, we don't need to copy God's Law with our hands or hang it by appendages on our clothing to have it near us; through Jesus, His code of righteousness is already in our hearts. His code alters our spiritual DNA. Any doubts? Just take a look at 2 Corinthians 5:17 where it says that anyone who accepts Jesus as Savior is a "new creature," and then Verse 20 says that this person has "the righteousness of God." God changes the code, or nature, in our spirits from sin and darkness to righteousness and light. This spiritual transformation is what enables His Spirit to be unified with ours. Darkness disappears because it cannot remain in the light.

One vivid experience I had with the power of light over darkness happened when my mom took me to a local cave for a tour. I was still in elementary school and *thought* I knew what darkness was before going, I mean, my bedroom got dark. Scary dark. However, that day, I realized how mistaken I was.

When we got into the belly of the cave, deep enough that the sunlight could no longer reach us, our tour guide had everyone turn off their flashlights. It felt like I was suddenly sucked in the vortex of a black hole. I kept blinking my eyes, unable to believe the incredible depths that darkness was able to obtain; yet the moment the guide turned on her light, the darkness dissipated. It didn't matter how dark the darkness was. It didn't matter how powerful it seemed. It had no power in the light. Wherever the light shone, it had to go.

It is the same in our lives. It doesn't matter how dark our lives were before Jesus. It doesn't matter how crushingly powerful darkness appears to be. Shadows have *no power* in Christ's light. And the darkness doesn't just take a backseat to His light, it vanishes the instant Jesus enters. One decision. One millisecond. Instant transformation. His Spirit is unified with ours and transforms our spirits into mirror images of Him. It's not slow. It's not timid. It's instantaneous and life-altering. And it's a done deal.

So, if God's power in our lives through spiritual unity is a done deal, why don't we see more of it? Why don't we experience more of it? Those questions bring us to the second part of the diagram. Our minds.

While the transformation of our spirits is an instantaneous gift, our minds are a completely different story. Our minds tend to drift toward the negative side of every single issue in life that we encounter, from our spouses, to peers, to situations at work or church, and the list could go on and on. It's a surprising observation that research has supported over and over again: people tend to think negatively about the world around them and remember the negative more than the positive.[33] How in the world are we going to accomplish what God has for us and experience the limitless freedom and joy He's *already given* to us if our minds are stuck in a gutter full of slimy trash? It's simple. We can't. And we won't.

In my opinion, the number one reason why we don't see more of God's power in our lives is because *we* short-circuit it. Our minds find the negative, and we focus on it. Maybe even obsess on it. I hate to admit it, but I've done this more times than I care to remember. The problem is, when we focus on the negative, we're focusing on the problem and not on the solution, which is always Jesus. Why else would God tell us to "take every thought captive to the obedience of Christ" in 2 Corinthians 10:5? After all, this is how we effectively wield those spiritual weapons that Paul wrote about in Verse 4 so we can live in God's power and victory.

We need to take responsibility for our thought life, align it with the Bible, and allow Him to fill us with His truth. Otherwise, we run the risk of short-circuiting our ability to allow God's power to work in our lives and to effectively wield that power to minister to others—and biblical gentleness remains elusive. It's so sad; so many of us are stuck focusing on the problem that we don't realize the way to escape this circle of negativity is closer than our fingertips. After all, God is the solution and, because of Jesus, God is in us. We just need to convince our minds to get in line with God's truth. That takes time, discipline, following the Holy Spirit's lead, and complete dependence upon Him.

Paul discusses this concept in Romans 12:2 when he writes, "Do not be conformed to this world, but be transformed by the renewing of your mind, so that you may prove what the will of God is, that which is good and acceptable and perfect." Mind renewal is a process, and not an overnight one. We are only able to fully comprehend the reality that is in our spirits when our minds are in line with God's truth. We can also only truly discern His nudges and His voice when our thoughts are in line with His. And how can we operate in the power of the Spirit if we cannot discern His leading? God does not simply allow people, even believers, to willy-nilly perform miracles by His hand! He unleashes His power through us as we are obedient to Him, and, according to this verse in Romans, the only way we can accurately follow His leading in our lives is by having our thought life in line with His truth. No wonder we need to control our minds! Imagine what would happen if Christians everywhere got their minds to line up with the Word and the Holy Spirit within them? Love. Signs. Wonders. Miracles! Why? Because *that* is what is in our spirits.

So, let's take a look at some of the slimy trash our minds can get too comfortable around, thereby short-circuiting God's power in our lives. One form of slime is self-focus. This can be obvious such as with selfishness and condescending judgments toward others, but it can also be insidious, namely through refusing to forgive and self-deprecation. How can unforgiveness be self-focus? I mean, wasn't it their fault?! Simple. By choosing to not forgive, we are focusing on our own injured feelings and not on God's redemptive power of love and gracious forgiveness. Forgiveness has *nothing* to do with the person who offended us or the wrongful action. Forgiveness also does *not* excuse wrongful behavior. Rather, the choice to forgive boils down to a heart issue and the atmosphere we want to maintain within our hearts and minds. Forgiveness has *everything* to do with releasing anger, resentment, and bitterness in exchange for God's love and joy as well as a deeper connection with the Lord. This is why God commands us to forgive over and over again (see Luke 17:3-4, Colossians 3:13 and Ephesians 4:31-32). In my life, every single time I find that I want to remain angry toward someone, I ask myself this question: "Is this offense worth losing my joy and putting a wedge between me and God?" The answer is always, "NO" and, inevitably, I release my hurt and anger before the Lord. If we choose anger, we choose self over our connection to the Lord and short-circuit God's power in our lives.

The slime of self-focus can be quite sneaky, as it also comes in the form of self-deprecation. Criticizing oneself is *not* humble, holy, or honorable; it is nothing short of destructive. Furthermore, self-deprecation takes the focus off of God and serving others and puts it right back on ourselves. We need to remember that God created us in His image, and this is exactly how we should see ourselves. If there be any doubt, just go to the Bible. It is loaded with verses containing God's truth about us (see Ephesians 2:10, Galatians 4:6-7, and 1 Peter 2:9 for starters). Focusing, and perhaps even meditating, on one of those Bible verses can help align our minds with God's truth and keep our minds from straying toward inappropriate self-focus (more on that in Chapter 8) so we can be effective ministers for the Lord.

Another type of slime many of us often encounter with our minds is doubt. Our minds' predilection toward doubt blocks God's power that resides within our spirits. As exemplified throughout both the Old and New Testaments, His power is unleashed through faith. Miracles such as the parting of the Red Sea, physical healings, and walking on water were all possible because someone chose faith over doubt.

Despite being completely illogical, Moses lifted his staff in front of the Red Sea. He exchanged what he saw and knew in the physical for what God promised, and God's power was manifested as the sea parted. Jesus said repeatedly that it was due to people's faith that they were healed. They weren't healed simply because Jesus was in the same area! This alone did not release His healing power; just look Bartimaeus's story in Mark 10:46-52. It took Bartimaeus's actions, driven by faith, to receive healing for his eyesight. This was confirmed in Verse 52 when Jesus says, "Go, your faith has made you well." Finally, Peter, the only discile to step out of the boat in faith on Jesus's call to come, was able to momentarily walk on water; it was only when he doubted that he began to sink (see Matthew 14:31).

Faith releases God's power and enables us to operate within His power.

Furthermore, it has been my experience that it is impossible to choose faith and remain negative. For me, choosing faith causes negative thoughts to melt away. As God's power bursts forth from His Spirit within me, it incinerates the negativity; negativity stands no chance in the presence of God. Darkness vanishes in the light.

Another strategy we can implement to overcome mind slime is to speak God's truth out loud. Romans 10:17 says, "Faith comes by hearing," Proverbs 18:21 says, "Death and life are in the power of the tongue," and Matthew 18:18 says, "Whatever you bind on earth will have been bound in heaven, and whatever you loose on earth will have been loosed in heaven." Therefore, by using our tongues to speak forth His Word, we are able to release His power of life, and there's a bonus: faith is generated in our hearts by hearing God's Word. What greater way to generate faith than by using our mouths to release His power in our lives? Finally, it's nearly impossible to think and speak different things simultaneously, which means that when we speak God's truth from His Word, those negative thoughts will be silenced. Immediately. This method may need to be implemented over and over again as these thoughts have a knack for finding their way back into our minds. But many find that if there's a struggle to silence unwanted thoughts, speaking God's truth is an effective, instantaneous solution. Therefore, both speaking *and* silently focusing on God's truth are two strategic weapons we can wield to combat mind slime and get ourselves back on track to walking in faith and God's power and cultivating biblical gentleness in our lives.

Bottom line: faith is in the realm of the mind. It is a decision. Faith aligns our minds with God's truth in our spirits. One decision, one moment of faith in Jesus, enabled our sinful spirits to transform into the righteousness of God. In that one moment, our minds aligned with God's truth, and power was released that changed our eternal destiny. Our minds need to accept and line up with God's truth. It is by maintaining this alignment of our minds through faith that God is able to accomplish His work in and through us. We need to choose faith in order to silence the doubts and negativity so we can experience the fullness of God's power in our lives. Notice, I said *choose*. This is an act of volition and should be a lifestyle for every Christian. Moment by moment, thought by thought, we need to *choose* to have our minds align with God's truth. It is only by living a lifestyle of faith that we are able to please God (see Hebrews 11:6).

The next link in the diagram of aligning ourselves to operate in God's power is the mouth, because what comes out of our mouths is a direct reflection of the appetite of our minds. Proverbs 4:23 says, "Watch over your heart with all diligence, for from it flow the springs of life." Yes, this verse says heart not mind, but this same exact word, *lebab*, also means "mind" and "bethinks themselves."[23] Furthermore, ancient Hebrew culture referred to the heart when referencing both the centers of intellect and of emotions.[16] So, in other words, this verse could also be read, "Watch over your mind and the way you think and feel about yourself with all diligence." Why keep a lockdown on it? Because whatever is in there will eventually break out, and usually the first way our thoughts escape is through our mouths.

Jesus reiterates the mind-mouth connection in Matthew 12:34 when He says, "For the mouth speaks out of that which fills the heart." Is it any wonder that the Bible commands us in Philippians 4:8 to think about "[w]hatever is true…honorable…right…pure…lovely… [and of] good repute, if there is any excellence and if anything worthy of praise, dwell on these things" instead of what is negative and toxic? The only way our words are going to be honorable, lovely, pure, and uphold a positive reputation is if that is where our mind dwells.

As human beings, we can only control the outward manifestation of our mind fodder so long. Eventually, it *will* spill out all over those around us. If our minds are focused on the negative, then our words and attitudes will be negative. But if instead we choose to focus on the positive, our words and attitudes will follow suit. Our mouths betray what our minds feed upon. It may be obvious. It could also be subtle. But it is there.

This brings us back to our original topic—being a conduit for God's power. If our words do not line up with God's truth, our conduit is short-circuited. We may have conquered doubts within our minds and have faith to see God move, but if our mouths are constantly spewing negativity and gossip, we're still short-circuiting the conduit. James 3:3-12 is pretty clear on this point: the tongue "defiles our entire body and sets the course of our life" in Verse 6 and Verses 9-11 say:

> *With it we bless our Lord and Father, and with it we curse men, who have been made in the likeness of God; from the same mouth come blessing and cursing. My brethren, things ought not to be this way.*

James goes on to say that when we behave this way, it is like we are living a duplicitous life; we are trying to be two totally different things. How can we be effective ministers for God, operating in His power when our mouths line up with opposing forces and are essentially undercutting those He loves? How can we expect our prayers to unleash God's power when we pray for God to touch someone and then turn around and gossip about that same person? James compares it to a fountain that attempts to provide both salt and fresh water. It's impossible. Holiness and purity cannot coexist with sin; light and darkness—it simply does not work. Our mouths need to line up with God's purity, or else we're mucking up the fountain. Muddy water is useless; we need to choose God's purification in our lives so we are powerful, effective ministers for the Lord.

Another common area that our mouths tend to falter in is complaining about our current life circumstances. This is a serious issue because it is tantamount to complaining about God's plan for our lives which is the same as doubting His plan and His goodness. God takes this very seriously— remember the Israelites? God placed them on a path through the desert to the Promised Land, and what did they do? They complained as shown in Numbers 14:2, "Would that we had died in the land of Egypt! Or…in this wilderness" and openly doubted as shown in Verse 3 of the same chapter, "Why is the Lord bringing us to this land, to fall by the sword?"

I imagine it was hard to maintain a positive attitude and faith in God's plan. The desert isn't exactly a pleasant place to be, even with modern conveniences. It had to be downright unbearable during the time of the Ancient Israelites, yet how did God respond to their complaining and doubt? Not with promises. Not with empowerment either. They were forced to wander in the desert for forty years! Forty years of short-circuited plans because of words which revealed attitudes that did not line up with His truth. He takes our words very seriously because words have power. After all, Jesus told us *twice* in Matthew that "whatever you bind on earth shall have been bound in heaven, and whatever you loose on earth shall have been loosed in heaven," once in 16:19 and again in 18:18. Our words have power—God-given power.

The bitterness of negativity, complaints, gossip, and open doubts cannot coexist with the fresh life found in God's truth. In order for our prayers to have the greatest impact, our words should be fresh, not bitter. They need to reflect the freshness of God everywhere and not just in the prayer closet. God takes our words seriously, and so should we. Our words should be full of God's life and truth at home, in the workplace, when we're running errands, and when we're relaxing with friends and family. I believe this is what James meant when he wrote in James 5:16 that "the effective prayer of a righteous man can accomplish much." Simply having faith will not open the floodgates of God's power in our prayer lives; our words need to speak God's grace and life. Renewing our minds is an important first step, but it is not the final key. As we renew our minds, the words of our mouths must be renewed as well. God's power flows best through a clear conduit…not one gunked up with buildup from words no better than sewage.

The final portion of living a life that allows God's power to flow through us so we can walk in biblical gentleness is the way we live our lives and our deeds. James 2:18 does an excellent, and blunt, job of describing the impact of our deeds by saying, "Faith without works is useless," and James supports this claim through the example of Abraham.

Despite living before defined righteousness and provision of both methods of achieving right standing before God, the Levitical Law and faith in Jesus, Abraham was deemed righteous. How? Because he verbalized his belief in God? No, it was more than that. Not only did he verbally profess his faith in God, he *lived* it. The choices he made, such as leaving all that he knew for a land he had never seen, demonstrated his internal beliefs. This principle of backing up what we say with our behavior spans generations and cultures. It is so true and timeless that there are two common clichés about it: *talk is cheap* and *actions speak louder than words* because the choices we make are evidence of what we truly believe in our hearts. But getting back to what the Bible says about this principle; James 1:23-24 says:

> *If anyone is a hearer of the word and not a doer, he is like a man who looks at his natural face in a mirror; for once he has looked at himself and gone away, he has immediately forgotten what kind of person he was.*

I'll be honest, for a while this verse confused me; I wondered how hearing the Bible and not living according to its principles correlated with viewing oneself in a mirror. Then it hit me.

When we believe in Jesus and accept His sacrifice, our spirits are instantly transformed, as previously discussed in this chapter. Because of this, when we read the Bible and listen to Scripture, the verses we read reflect back to us the reality that is in our spirits. If we as Christians want to know what our spirits look like, we should read the Bible. Therefore, if our actions do not line up with biblical principles, we are behaving in a way that is contrary to the eternal part of who we are. We've forgotten what we look like. We've forgotten that within our spirits reside holiness, love, joy, power, gentleness, and peace among many other godly qualities.

Obviously, we live in an imperfect world, and our spirits reside within our flesh. We cannot expect ourselves to always make the perfect choice, but we *can* choose to abide in the Lord and live by His principles. There is a difference between simply making a mistake and choosing a lifestyle that is repugnant to the Lord; shortcomings and mistakes can and will happen, but our lifestyles should be sweet to Him. Even Abraham, the example of righteousness through faith demonstrated by actions provided by James, made errors in judgment that, unfortunately for him, have been recorded for every human being to read for thousands of years. One such example is found in Genesis 20 where Abraham lies about Sarah being his wife and gives her away to Abimelech. Fortunately, God gave Abimelech a dream and Sarah was returned to Abraham, untouched. Despite errors in judgment such as this, Abraham was still considered righteous because his *lifestyle* was one that demonstrated his faith in God.

If our lifestyles do not reflect godliness, and we repeatedly ignore the promptings of His Spirit, we create an effective block against His power working in and through our lives. We can attend church regularly, sing the songs, listen to the sermons, pray, and read the Bible, but if we consistently make choices that conflict with Scripture and/or refuse to obey His leading in our lives, God's power will not flow through us properly. We've plugged up our vessels.

If what is culturally accepted and expected is in conflict with biblical principles, ditch it. We need to take off the lids, remove the plugs, and straighten out the kinks in our lives caused by godless beliefs and systems. We need to mobilize our faith. How? Show it. Live it. One decision at a time. One act at a time. One by one, our choices add up. They add up to a lifestyle, a lifestyle that allows *us* to be effective conduits of God's power.

In summary, in order to be an effective instrument of God's power and take an important step toward developing gentleness in our lives, our spirits must be unified with God and our minds, mouths, and lives need to be in alignment with His truth. They all need to align with God's principles, not just one or two.

It sounds so easy, but the reality is, it can be downright difficult to achieve this. Actually, I'd say in and of ourselves, it's impossible. Believe me, I've tried. I spent many years trying to modify my behavior and my words and struggled. And failed. And got frustrated. And overwhelmed. And depressed. Modifying behavior is effortful, difficult, and time-consuming. And the worst part is that, in my experience, it did nothing to alter my words or my mind. I spent years feeling like I was spinning in perpetual cycles, spiraling further and further into hopelessness. Then I discovered that if I could allow *God* to do it, *not me*, it would save me a lot of headache, heartache, and I would be able to achieve my goal. For me, attempting to modify from the outside in did not work, but God, working from the inside out, accomplished miracles.

It all boiled down to the fact that I had to stop trying. That was the secret. I got myself out of the way, and this change of process revolutionized my approach. Instead of struggling through tedious and ineffective behavior modification programs that I created for myself, I gave up. Instead, I ditched my behavioral modification programs and decided to pray, read the Bible, worship, and meditate on Scripture daily. What happened shocked me. I could not believe how quickly my mind began to align with biblical principles by simply allowing God to take control. Once my mind was in tune with the Lord, my words and actions followed suit; it was almost effortless...well, at least compared to what I had been doing. And that conclusion makes sense, since our minds control what flows from our mouths and lives. We do not act or speak without it germinating in our minds first.

When I surrendered to God, I temporarily got my flesh-driven mind out of the way. This allowed my spirit to commune, unfettered, with His Spirit which in turn enabled His influence to grow and dominate since I was focused on *Him* not *me*. I needed to refocus onto the solution, which was, and always is, Jesus. By focusing on Him, I became more like Him. When I focused on my behavior, I became more like, well, my behavior. Since then, I've come to think of this method as working from the inside out, and I've found it to be the most effective and efficient way to help me to be more like Him. It makes complete sense, of course, God knows exactly how to mold us and help us grow, and He knows exactly what environment conducts His power best. So, why not just let Him create what He wants us to be? We need to focus on Him, follow His lead, and allow Him to do the work.

As I mentioned in the preface, this book began as a Bible study lesson on the fruit of the Spirit I created for my daughters. When I came to gentleness, I thought this was the one fruit that I was naturally gifted in—I mean, I had been told that I had a gentle spirit my whole life. As soon as I realized that gentleness contained great power, I realized that yet again, outside of God's supernatural power, my life was lacking.

What others perceived as gentleness was not a smoothie of great power, self-control, and kindness; it was fear, timidity, and insecurity. In droves. I could barely look another person in the eye without a dried-out, sticky mouth, sweaty palms, gonging heart, and knocking knees. Growing up I got really good at shrinking into walls and furniture and leaned on friends and family to speak up for me, and when I went to graduate school for speech-language pathology, it was difficult for me to say a simple, "Hello," to patients and their families. I hate to say it, but that was my supervisor's goal for me—to say hello. And I was even married already! So as you read the rest of this chapter, which highlights the developing research about power in relationships and what contributes to a sense of power, please know that I am writing this for myself as well.

Social hierarchies have been around pretty much as long as human beings have roamed the Earth. It didn't take long for dominant personalities to exert power and begin to take control and establish authority—ancient kings, emperors, and pharaohs come to mind. Some personalities just exude more power and perceived dominance than others and make leading look like a piece of cake. These are people that just fill a room with their presence, command attention, and incur followers. They may even be able to do this before uttering a single word…but how?

It all starts with presentation. Have you ever had a gut feeling or an impression about someone before you even shook hands or said hello? This is because our brains automatically process social information before our centers of reasoning and logic kick in, and this is especially true when it comes to perceiving dominance.[25,32] It may be unfair, because short of plastic surgery it is completely uncontrollable, but the appearance of your face contributes significantly to first impressions and to the perception of power.[4,28] To be more specific, if the bone structure of your face creates a shape with greater width relative to height, you are perceived as being more powerful.[4,34] Additionally, mature and lower-pitched voices are associated with greater dominance.[27,35] Fortunately, despite these physiological perceptions, the perception of power is not entirely automatic and God-given.

Allow me to explain. The first area we can control when it comes to power perception is the way we dress. Whether or not we like it, agree with it, or even care, the way we put our wardrobes together sends a message to those around us and can impact the way others perceive us. Dr. Robert Cialdini, a leader in the study of how persuasion works, wrote about the power of attire in his book, *Influence* and in this book he discusses the impact of clothing on behavior. For example, by simply wearing a security guard uniform, a man was able to persuade significantly more people to do things, from picking up trash to giving someone else a dime, compared to when he wasn't wearing the uniform. If wearing a uniform isn't an option, or desired, don't worry because the author's examples weren't limited to uniforms; he also provided an example of research done involving well-tailored business suits. This study found that three-and-a-half *times* as many people followed someone wearing a well-tailored business suit into the street *against* the traffic light compared to the same person wearing street clothes.[7] The take-away? If we want an effective way to boost our image of power to those around us, we should spend a few extra moments (and possibly dollars) on our wardrobes. Simply wearing professional attire increases others' perceptions of our power status and increases our influence with those around us.

A second area we can control is our voices. Ever notice that when exerting authority, voices tend to get just a little bit louder and lower? I know I have. This is because a voice that has a lower pitch and higher volume is perceived as containing greater power. Other qualities correlated with vocal power include greater variability in the use of tones and inflections. In other words, a voice that is dynamic and allowed to rise and fall, is perceived as having greater power.[27,31,35]

A third controllable power projector is body language. Studies show that people perceived as having power tend to exhibit postures that are considered dominant. Dominant postures include those that make someone look broader and taller, such as widespread limbs, hand and arm gesturing, standing tall and erect, and standing in a more visible position relative to others.[11,15] Additional dominant behaviors identified by research include relaxed facial expressions, such as direct eye contact and less tension in the mouth.[3,7,14] Adapting postures such as these, I believe, go to the primal, instinctual drive within us; that drive that makes us want to follow the person who appears strongest, most competent, and most confident.

Furthermore, some studies have shown that adopting these higher power postures and characteristics can actually help someone *feel* more powerful. By simply having subjects hold a power pose using expansive, open body postures for two minutes, researchers found an impact on hormone levels.[11] Specifically, they found that testosterone, which is associated with dominance, was elevated and cortisol, which is associated with stress and lower power, was decreased.[6] Another study showed that holding these poses can improve self-esteem and energy.[5] Not convinced? Dr. Li Huang, a researcher from Northwestern University, and colleagues have conducted studies and found that those who held dominant postures were the ones that ended up with powerful thoughts and behaviors—not those who were actually placed in authoritative roles.[18] *Still* not convinced? The influence of holding dominant postures was shown to be effective by providing a measurable performance boost for a pretty important real-life situation—the job interview.[10]

Whether or not one is interviewing for a job or hoping for a promotion, having self-confidence is key to improving what is called *presence*.[14] In her book, *The Power of Presence*, leadership coach Kristi Hedges discusses the importance of "intentional presence," or choosing how others will perceive you. She discusses choosing positive, optimistic thoughts to promote confidence. The reason? Because our brains are like dirt roads, and just like dirt roads, the more we track down the same path in our brains, the more worn that path gets. The more worn it gets, the faster and easier those particular thoughts will fly around our brains, which means those thought patterns become very hard to break.[17] And she's not the only one who has written about the impact of our thought life.

Dr. Cialdini also places emphasis on thoughts and attention in his book, *Pre-suasion,* where he asserts that the power of what we focus our minds on is so powerful that it has the ability to influence our judgments and actually cause events to occur. The kicker? This process is automatic.[8] Therefore we may not even be aware it is happening! Is it any wonder why God would admonish us in Philippians 4:8 to think about things that are true, honorable, right, pure, and lovely? He knows that what we focus our minds on shapes our decisions and who we eventually become. Even if we don't consciously recognize it!

A great first step to improving confidence and aligning our thoughts with God's truth is to take a hard look at these thoughts, also known as our self-talk. It isn't always easy to recognize the lies we may be telling ourselves because if we tell ourselves the same lie over and over again for years, our brain thinks it's true and will find verification of this "truth" everywhere we go. Notice, I said our brains will *find* verification not that there actually *is* verification. Take a moment to let that sink in. There's a big difference between *valid* truths and *perceived* truths about ourselves. Valid truth is found in the Bible, perceived truths are founded on nothing but what our own minds conjure up—and that can be downright dangerous. If our thoughts are not in line with what Scripture says is true, then it's a lie, and it needs to be replaced with the truth.

I spent many years struggling with varying levels of depression. Even after God convinced me to continue my life here on Earth when I was a teenager, I still had horrible self-esteem which destroyed my confidence. Since I didn't like myself, subconsciously I couldn't truly believe that anyone else liked me. Approaching life with this mindset caused my insecurity meter to be off the charts. I struggled to approach others and always felt alone. I could be in a room full of people, even friends and family, and feel completely isolated. I also always felt that whatever I did was subpar compared to what everyone else could do. Those two lie-driven mindsets—I am alone and have nothing of value to offer anyone anyway—worked together to lead me to a place of utter darkness in my mind.

Then one day I had an "Aha!" moment. I realized that every morning I woke up and had this thought, "I'm depressed. I hate my life." This wasn't a conscious thought; it wasn't something that I spent time conjuring up or pondering. But it was there—subtle but there. When I realized that I started each day with this negative self-talk, I knew what I had to do: replace the negative with the positive. Since this thought process and the feelings that came with it had become automatic and subconscious, replacing them was easier said than done. In order to eradicate this thought and stop this self-defeating cycle, I had to intentionally wake up each morning and choose to think, "Thank You, Lord, for this day, a brand-new day for me to love You, serve You, and experience all the wonderful things You have for me today. Thank You for this gift." Once I became intentional and started practicing, each day became just a little bit easier, and my thoughts and attitudes were reshaped. I became more positive and was able to experience the Lord's joy in my heart, but it took self-awareness, discipline, time, and valid truth provided by Scripture to spark these changes.

Taking the steps required to remove the lies we believe and replace it with God's truth is a great place to start on the journey of walking in empowerment. Walking in power ultimately comes down to our thought lives and belief systems. But wait...isn't power a bad thing? After all, there is that bit of classic wisdom from Lord Acton that tells us "power tends to corrupt, and absolute power corrupts absolutely" and that "power demoralizes."[1] Prior to researching for this book, I had always agreed with Lord Acton, and history is replete with examples to support it: Napoleon, Caesar, Hitler— shall I continue? Then I read a bold statement by Harvard researcher, Dr. Amy Cuddy.

In her book, *Presence: Bringing Your Boldest Self to Your Biggest Challenges*, Dr. Cuddy makes the assertion that power does not corrupt. Yes, yes, we have all those historical examples, but no, power *itself* does not corrupt. It reveals. Wait. Hold up. Back up. What was that? *Power reveals.*[9] Research has shown that power does not change who the person is, rather, it improves confidence, which makes an individual more likely to take action.[2] Therefore, having power enables us to reveal ourselves, and without the confidence boost from power, vulnerability—and therefore connection—often remains an unconquered challenge. Furthermore, due to the confidence engendered by power, power improves our creativity, problem solving skills, abstract thinking abilities, and reduces the pressure we feel from circumstances around us.[13,21,29,30] Therefore, power enables us to make better decisions, take the steps needed to implement them, and experience less stress during the process.[30] Hmmm...I could see how this could go very wrong if a person was corrupt inside...but what if a person *isn't* corrupt? In that case, there are even more potential benefits to power.

For instance, having a sense of power also helps us focus on others rather than ourselves.[19] Focusing on others is crucial to fulfill God's call to live a life of gentleness, love, and service toward others. It is also important for our own mental health since self-focus is often associated with both depression and anxiety, both of which are associated with low power.[24] Interestingly, Dr. Ewa Kacewicz and colleagues from the University of Texas have done research on the use of the word "I" and found that people who frequently use the word "I" tend to have lower social power.[20]

Furthermore, power, in the absence of selfishness and corruption, was shown to increase our ability to understand others and what they feel. This surprising result from a research series led by Dr. Marianne Mast from the University of Neuchatel was consistent over four consecutive, related studies that had hundreds of participants.[24] Another shocking discovery was made by Dr. Johan Karremans and Dr. Pamela Smith. These two researchers collaborated on an intriguing mission to study the relationship of power and forgiveness. They gathered nearly 400 participants over a series of three consecutive, related studies and found that possessing power was associated with a greater degree of forgiveness and reduced rumination (persistent negative thoughts about a situation).[22] Dr. Cuddy asserted in her book that power enables us to connect, and after looking through the research, I'd have to agree. Power enables us to focus on and understand others, truly forgive when needed, have the confidence required to be vulnerable to others, and take action when circumstances demand it. Power reveals, power connects, and power enables us to be effective ministers of the Lord. No wonder gentleness contains great power.

Challenge Questions:

1. What negative thoughts have I allowed in my mind? Is there a pattern to the occurrence of these negative thoughts? If so, write it down.
2. What truth or truths can I replace these thoughts with?
3. How will I go about changing my thought patterns? Create a specific plan (refer back to the chapter as necessary for suggestions).
4. Are my words positive and uplifting? Do I express contentment and gratitude? How often do I complain? What steps can I take to express gratitude and contentment instead of complaining?
5. Are my thoughts and words full of faith or doubt? Which areas of my life do I struggle to walk in faith? What steps can I take to walk in faith and not fear and doubt? Make these specific but

attainable (for example, praying out loud, praying for someone to be healed, obeying the Lord's nudge whenever it happens and wherever you may be).

6. Are there areas in my life (thoughts, words, or behaviors) that I have refused to align with biblical truth and principles? If so, take time to lay these down before the Lord in repentance. Suggestion: find someone you trust that you can confess to and also an accountability partner (can be the same person) to help you stay on track in aligning your life with biblical truths and principles.

7. How do others currently perceive me? Why might they think this way? (You may need input from spouse, friends, neighbors, and coworkers.)

8. How do I want to be perceived by others? Why? What benefits for myself and others are there to being perceived in this way?

9. If there is a discrepancy between #7 and #8, what steps can I take to project the presence I want?

An Overview of Leadership

As already mentioned earlier in this book, leadership is one aspect of biblical gentleness. That being said, the topic of leadership is broad and far surpasses the scope of this book. There are a multitude of books and seminars that cover this topic in greater depth than what I will discuss here. Even though I've only included what I consider an overview of this topic, the volume of information warranted dividing this particular chapter into four sections. Each section covers a subtopic of leadership and its contribution to gentleness and contains self-reflective challenge questions.

It almost goes without saying that power and leadership go hand in hand more often than not. By default, leaders have power in that they make decisions that directly impact their subordinates; however, not all leaders are equally effective. What makes one leader beloved and another dreaded? How does one leader inspire others while another oppresses? Much of it boils down to leadership style and what is referred to as emotional intelligence.

What comes to mind when you think of a leader? Strength? Decisiveness? Is this person aloof or approachable? Enviable? The list could go on and on. Leaders problem solve, coordinate, and facilitate execution of tasks and are found in every social situation from the home to churches to businesses. Sometimes they are labelled (i.e., manager, CEO, or pastor), but sometimes they are not. Dr. Daniel Goleman, a leader on the topic of emotional intelligence, wrote a book entitled *Primal Leadership: Learning to Lead with Emotional Intelligence*, where he acknowledges that there are times that the designated, official leader is not the person who is actually leading. He goes on to explain that if the group has lost faith in the official leader, oftentimes another leader will arise from the group, and he calls this person the "emotional leader." This person is the one who sets the emotional tone for the group and eventually becomes the dominant individual.[15] This person's leadership may be unspoken and subtle, but it is present.

I once experienced exactly this situation. At one time, I had a manager who travelled from site to site and, when she was at our building, I rarely saw her leave the office to connect with the team. Over time, more and more distance grew between her and the team, and during this time another leader, an emotional leader, arose. This person stepped in and managed various administrative tasks for everyone and, before long, everyone looked to her for answers and direction. From there, she wound up setting the tone for the office; although she never stepped into an official leadership role, her connection to the team remained strong, and her opinions carried weight. And what happened to the official manager? Volitionally transferred.

Leaders that inspire are leaders that connect. Dr. Goleman uses the term "resonance or resonant leadership" for this quality.[15] The manager from my example above was not nasty; she was just distant, perhaps overworked and pulled in too many directions; but whatever the reason, it impacted her ability to connect with her staff. Dr. Goleman would most likely say that she lacked resonance with her staff, as she was unable to connect on an emotional level with the rest of the group. Her lack of connection with the staff did not make her a difficult boss, one whose demands are unreasonable, and who is completely inflexible to change. Her lack of resonance was also totally unlike a nasty boss, the one who yells, belittles, and verbally scourges the staff.

It is unfortunate that negative leaders will most likely continue to emerge as they have for millennia. Perhaps it is because history is replete with the innately powerful rising to the top, whether or not that person actually possesses the personal character development and people skills needed to perform the role with excellence. Typically, when we see these domineering, negative leaders, they are using styles of leadership that are termed *pacesetting* and *coercive* or *commanding*.[15]

The pacesetting style of leadership holds high performance expectations and requires that everything be done faster and better. This type of leader isn't afraid to call out those who don't meet his or her demands. Coercive/commanding leaders are slightly different in that they will dole out commands with little to no explanations and exact punishments for disobedience or incompetence.[15] It seems to make sense to have someone who sets high performance expectations and quality standards and isn't afraid to bark orders in a leadership position. It appears that this type of person would efficiently squeeze the best out of those around him/her and that recognition and rewards would follow this leader wherever he/she would go. I'm very glad, however, to say that studies have shown that this isn't the case. Fortunately, research is changing long-held mindsets of what effective leadership looks like.[15,30,31,32,33]

While both the pacesetting and coercive/commanding leadership styles can be harmless and successful when used with caution in the right situations, oftentimes they are overused and result in resentful subordinates and tense atmospheres.[15] My experience is that this generally results in miserable staff that just go through the motions, and there is a greater likelihood of lower quality work and higher staff turnover.[5] Obviously, this is bad for business. So, if the styles of leadership that we have commonly thought of as being the most effective are actually full of pitfalls, then what does effective leadership look like?

There are many labels for leadership styles that generate harmony and teamwork. Some of the popular labels are *transformational leadership*, *servant leadership*, *democratic leadership*, and *empowering leadership*. The literature on these styles is vast, so I will not parse out the differences between them in this book. Instead, I will just lump them all together under the umbrella term *positive leadership styles*.

Challenge Questions:

1. What traits contribute to successful teamwork? Successful leadership? Compare/contrast the two. Are there traits I possess from one or both? Are there positive traits I would like to have but do not at this time? Choose one positive trait and create a plan to begin cultivating it.
2. Think of a time when you collaborated with others. Was it successful? If it was, what specific elements do I believe contributed to its success? If not, what specific elements do I believe contributed to its lack of success?

Positive Leadership Styles

In the previous section, I mentioned two terms used by Dr. Goleman: resonance and resonant leadership. The English word resonance comes from the Latin word *resonantia*, which means "echo" and *resonare* which means to "resound;" *resound* means to "sound loudly, reverberate, to produce a sonorous or echoing sound." [28,29] I found Dr. Goleman's use of the term resonance in relationships interesting since I had learned about resonance as it related to sound when I was a speech-language pathology student.

Basically, resonance occurs when two items vibrate at the same frequency, and the easiest way I've found to experience resonance is the age-old trick of listening for the ocean inside a shell. The ocean sound we hear is actually miniscule sound waves that are vibrating right along with the walls of the hard shell. This causes the sound to be amplified, or to become louder, and enables us to hear some of the sounds around us that are too soft for us to hear on our own.[20,27] This is resonance. But resonance isn't limited to tiny sound waves and sea shells. Resonance can be intense and result in a powerful force—powerful enough to collapse a bridge.[11] Resonance occurs when two different items vibrate together on the same wavelength which results in greater power generation than when each item vibrates separately. Dr. Goleman got it right; I can't think of a better term for positive leadership than resonance.

This ability for a positive leader to resonate, to lead in a way as to produce greater results together as opposed to separately, is a central component to gentleness. Positive leadership styles are able to generate an atmosphere where creativity proliferates, team members flourish, and productivity booms.[4,15,25,30,33] Most often it is the leader that sets the tone for the rest of the group, since all eyes are typically on the leader. Leaders also tend to speak up first and speak more than the rest of the team, and their opinions are often valued more than anyone else's.[15] In business situations, studies have shown that when the leader is positive and satisfied with his or her job, there is a direct, positive impact to subordinates.[26,33] One study investigated over 300 store managers who had a total of over 1,600 subordinates and found that the managers' positive attitude and job satisfaction were directly and significantly related to positive attitudes and job satisfaction in their employees. They further investigated whether or not customers of these stores were also influenced by this effect, and indeed, found a direct, positive impact on customers as well.[26] Therefore, when the leader is positive, the team is much more likely to be positive and resonance often occurs. But what consistently contributes the most to this productive, harmonious atmosphere?

As I read through books and research on the various leadership styles, I found some common threads among them that I strongly suspect contribute to the success of each individual style. These include the following characteristics of the leader: warmth, humility, honesty, and genuine listening to others.[15,25,26,31,32] According to the literature I read, these attributes tend to result in the following: trust, confidence, and growth, both individually and as a team.[4,15,25,26,31,32] The rest of the chapter will explore these characteristics and their impact.

It is my opinion that a leader's warmth is essential to creating a positive team environment. Without leader warmth, trust and confidence are much less likely to develop. When confidence and trust are lacking, it is likely that communication is lacking too. If communication is lacking, it is likely that genuine listening is lacking as well. And honesty? That's probably suffering also. Therefore, warmth must come first. Literally. A leader's first impression should be one of warmth. This may feel counterintuitive, since we want our leaders to be strong and powerful. However, if the leader barges in with strength and competence only, alienation of subordinates is likely. Fortunately for leaders, though, studies such as those led by Dr. Bogdan Wojciszke have repeatedly shown that characteristics consistent with warmth are processed more quickly than those consistent with competence.[6,34,35] Therefore, if warm competence is presented, warmth will likely be the team's first impression.

First impressions are made in an instant, in that initial split-second when we see someone from across the room or hear their voice. We make these judgments automatically and adjust them as we deem necessary over the course of our interactions. And warmth as a first impression is correlated with perceptions of kindness, humility, and honesty.[6] But how do we make sure our first foot forward is warm?

Oftentimes having what is considered a "babyface" contributes to perceived warmth.[1,2] Similarly, voices can contribute to a first impression of warmth. One study asked participants to judge voices as being either "mature" or "babyish." Interestingly, they found that voices judged to be "babyish" were considered "warm," and the voices that were considered warm were strongly correlated with measures of "social closeness."[1] It almost seems unfair, since a chunk of what creates our first impressions is based upon our anatomy but, fortunately, there is more to first impressions than the way we look and the sound of our voices and, I'm glad to say, it's 100% under our control—our actions.

Actions consistent with warmth toward others, such as a genuine smile and avoiding arm crossing, can go a long way toward warming up a first impression.[6] Researchers have found that warm actions toward others promotes the release of oxytocin, which is well-known for its role in our ability to bond with others.[6] Therefore, when a leader demonstrates characteristics of warmth, the team is most likely being prepared for social connection on a physiological, chemical level, which according to Dr. Goleman, is key for an effective leader and highly successful teams.[6,14,15,16]

Not only is warmth a crucial attribute for a positive leader, but so are humility and honesty. Since humility will be discussed at length in Chapter 8, honesty will be explored next in this chapter. The Bible is very clear on the honesty issue. Over and over again, we are not just encouraged, we are commanded to tell the truth. Being an honest person can be costly at times, but, eventually, the price of lying will bankrupt us every time. Telling the truth, even when it's difficult, not only protects our reputations in the long run but, in my experience, it also safeguards relationships.

When I was young, I had what I thought was a great friend. We were always at one of our houses, giggling and squealing together, playing games and inventing new ones. Then one day, through a mutual friend, I heard some stories she told about me. This mutual friend was angered by what I had supposedly said and done and was confronting me about it. None of it was true, and it took some doing to convince her of this. However, when I confronted who I thought was my "great" friend, she adamantly denied the allegations.

Shortly after this, more rumors she had spread about other people surfaced, and of course, none of those were true either. This further affirmed my gut instinct that she had lied to me, and I felt betrayed. Her lying not only hurt my relationship with our mutual friend, but it destroyed my relationship with her. The foundation of trust we had built was obliterated. Since I could no longer trust her, I began avoiding her, and our friendship imploded into a black hole of distant memories. Lying may appear to help us achieve our goals in the short-term, but in the long-term it *will* exact compensation, drain our resources, and demand more. It's just not worth it.

Lack of honesty and integrity not only takes its toll on personal relationships, but its dirty work is seen in the business realm as well. Dr. Cialdini wrote about the impact of unethical leadership in his book, *Pre-suasion*, and made the assertion that employees who are under unethical leadership tend to feel greater amounts of stress. This in turn leads to poorer work performance and higher turnover rates. He went on to provide one estimate: if a midsize firm of 1,000 employees lost 10% of their workers, the total turnover cost would be about $4 million dollars. And furthermore, even if employees remain in a company with unethical leadership, fraud tends to run rampant in these businesses and bad public relations are a high probability.[5] The financial ramifications of fraudulent business practices and the resulting bad public relations cannot be underestimated. Slime. It oozes all the way down, from the top to the bottom.

As it turns out, at one time I worked for a company where fraud was rampant, and by God's grace, got out unscathed. I once had an on-call job for a company that provided rehabilitation services in a local nursing home. I had originally gotten the job through a recommendation from a friend and, right after I started, all was well. But then things started to change. The boss left, and the company that originally hired me lost the contract at the facility.

This new company appointed a new boss, and that's when the real shifting happened. I noticed that coworkers who had been at that facility for many years started to leave, and the ones that remained grumbled all the live-long day. Then one day, as I was sitting in the office completing the day's documentation, the second-in-command asked me to clock out…immediately.

I was surprised, as I had clearly just fired up the computer and hadn't even begun to type. But I complied with his request, shocked that I was being directed to work off the clock. I think it took me at least another twenty minutes to complete my paperwork. The kicker? The assistant manager was in the office the entire time. In that moment, my trust in the company was broken and, as a result, I offered fewer and fewer hours.

Eventually, this company lost the contract at the facility, and I decided it was a good time to cut ties. I later found out that I was not the only one expected to work off the clock; the entire department was forced to do so— on a regular basis! I also learned later of other instances of fraud that occurred throughout the company. Needless to say, this particular company no longer exists—thankfully! Clearly, consistent and continued dishonesty eventually exacted its compensation from this particular company.

Another facet of honesty is *authenticity,* which society defines as being true to who you are and acting according to your true feelings.[14] In my opinion, as Christians, we should be taking this definition with a bit of salt— biblical salt. As Christians we know that our thoughts and emotions don't always *quite* line up with Scriptural principles. It is my belief, that as Christians, we should *first* line up our minds and emotions with the Bible *then* behave in a way that is consistent with His truth. And *that* is authenticity at its best! Keep this in mind as we delve into what the secular research has to say about authenticity.

Ever been around someone syrupy sweet? Someone you just *knew* had an ulterior motive? How about that plastic, pasted-on smile? What about those gut feelings we get when we just feel like something is somehow off? These perceptions occur because there are incredibly fast and subtle signs of inauthenticity which are provided by facial expressions or body language that, in my opinion, *require* the automatic processing of our brain. Why? These physiological betrayals amount to all of a microsecond-long flash and are processed automatically by our brains thanks to our tiny but mighty amygdalas.[14,16]

As I read through the literature on this topic, it seemed as though researchers struggled with developing and establishing exact parameters for this phenomenon. Instead, most experts in the field tended to label it as "asynchrony," and described a variety of forms this can take, such as asymmetrical facial expressions, faltering expressions that don't appear and disappear smoothly, or maybe something is just "off" about the way the body is held.[7,9] This is because being inauthentic is on par with projecting a lie about oneself.[7,12] Therefore, when we deceive, it "leaks" and can result in sweaty palms, an almost imperceptible flicker in our eye, a split-second twitch, or a subtle adjustment in the way we speak. Bottom line: our brains know our lies and will tell on us every time.[7,19] The way God designed our brains is astounding! The instantaneous, automatic processing of our brains goes beyond what science can quantify and is undeniably beneficial when navigating social situations.

Ultimately, it does not matter what cues we subconsciously provide that alert others to our inauthenticity. What matters is that inauthenticity undermines trust, which is crucial in personal and professional relationships. Perhaps it is a safeguard against manipulation, but, thanks to our amygdala's automatic processing, our brains tend to be pretty good (but not always perfect) at discerning when someone is not genuine. The result? Those who behave like they are constantly performing on stage are not trusted. Taking off the costumes, makeup, and masks to reveal one's true self can be tough, but it is the only way to build trust and true connections.

Trust is the foundation upon which every single other facet of relationships is built upon and without it, hobgoblins of insecurity, suspicion, and resentment run rampant. Kristi Hedges writes in her book, *The Power of Presence*, that in order to promote an atmosphere of trust, each individual must begin by demonstrating their own trustworthiness.[18] In other words, if we expect trust to develop in our relationships, we must first be trustworthy ourselves. And trustworthiness is especially crucial for leaders, since they set the tone for the entire team and an atmosphere of trust helps create an effective, productive team. I would furthermore say that this entire process of becoming trustworthy begins when we become an authentic person. Therefore, a gentle leader must lead from a place of authenticity; it builds trust and bridges the divide between management and staff which increases communication and cooperation.[6]

In order to be authentic, an individual must first be aware of personal goals and values *and be willing to act on them*. Once personal authenticity is achieved, the leader must also tune into the dynamics of the group. After bringing these factors together, the whole team can become dynamite.[15,16] In my experience, these are the teams with a passionate leader whose enthusiasm spreads throughout the team, electrifying them with inspiration and motivation.

My first boss after graduate school was one such leader. I remember the interview vividly. I had had back-to-back interviews in the city, suburbs, and coal country; as a broke college student, all I wanted was a job. I had just had an interview at a posh hospital near Philadelphia, and as I pulled into this, the last facility, I could tell right away that I was no longer at a high-end hospital.

The manager met me at the reception area and took me back to the department for the interview. We sat on hard, metal folding chairs in an under-lit supply closet that happened to have a computer. This was her office. However, after talking with her for just a few minutes, I knew this was the job I was going to take. Why? It certainly wasn't the luxurious office suite. It wasn't the pay either; her company had already been outbid by a competitor. It was her.

Something about her was special. Something about her made me want to work with her and for her and give her my best. She was a warm and authentic leader. She was upbeat, up front, and made me feel like I belonged there. Under her management, I grew and flourished as a person and as a therapist. I gave her my best; I went to the moon and back for her. During my first review, she wrote that I had management potential and offered to assist my climb. I had every intention to do so. But then came the wrench.

One day, she transferred to another facility and then I transferred elsewhere. Despite this, my plans for ascent into management were continuing to percolate in my mind; my new boss was every bit as authentic, warm, and resonant as the last one. I continued to grow in confidence and gain skills. Remember that wrench? Here it comes. The company restructured. My facility was placed into a different territory and a new upper management team came with it.

This new team didn't win my trust and heart the way the last team had. Instead of building authentic connections, they made us feel the divide between management and staff, with higher productivity demands on staff therapists and special manager-and-up-only off-site perks. Suspicion and resentment began to run rampant in the department. I still did my job and enjoyed it, but I no longer made those treks to the moon and back. Since I no longer trusted upper management, I no longer wanted to be in management. My motivation and aspirations became a blackened wick, a memory of goals that had been extinguished into nothingness. I went from planning my moves into the upper realms of the company to punching a time clock as a staff therapist.

Challenge Questions:

1. What characteristics do I associate with warmth? Do I possess these characteristics? Enlist the help of friends, family, and coworkers if needed.

2. What can I do to show more warmth to those around me?

3. What characteristics do I associate with trustworthiness? Do I possess these characteristics? Enlist the help of friends, family, and coworkers if needed.

4. What can I do to demonstrate more trustworthiness to those around me? Make a specific plan.

5. Do I maintain a lifestyle of authenticity, integrity, and honesty? What steps do I need to take, if any, to begin or fine-tune this type of lifestyle?

6. Am I confident in my abilities and ideas? If not, why? What steps can I take to experience greater confidence?

7. Think of a successful leader—this can be from the business world or perhaps a church or family. List specific traits and actions that contribute to his/her success.

8. Are there any qualities consistent with positive leadership that I feel I either do not possess or lack confidence in? Develop a plan to begin cultivating and using this trait, when appropriate.

Godly Leadership

The Bible has many examples of leaders who mobilized a group of followers and make a positive impact; Joseph, Moses, Joshua, Nehemiah, Peter, and Paul all come to mind. By obeying the Lord, these men were able to feed nations, lead Israel out of bondage and into the Promised Land, rebuild Israel's wall, and grow the Christian church. But they did not do all of these amazing works by themselves; they needed a team, a team that was inspired by a leader who was inspired by God.

Godly leadership begins with a leader who is in full submission to the Lord. This leader must have a genuine relationship with God and follow God's leading and vision for his or her life. When a leader has a true connection with God and shares God's vision with the team, it helps foster trust and inspiration in the team members. And as we've seen, trust and inspiration often result in growth, creativity, and productivity...and that's from secular research. Now imagine adding God's direction and power into the mix. We would be unstoppable! Let's take a closer look at one such unstoppable biblical leader—Jesus.

Jesus was, and always will be, the perfect example of a gentle, positive, godly leader. First, He was fully submitted to the Lord and obeyed God's leading at each and every step. He said so Himself in John 5:19, "Truly, truly I say to you, the Son can do nothing of Himself, unless it is something He sees the Father doing; for whatever the Father does, these things the Son also does in like manner." Jesus, being fully submitted to the Father, received greater depths of revelation and inspiration from the Father's heart, as we see in Verse 20 of the same chapter when He says, "For the Father loves the Son, and shows Him all things that He Himself is doing." It was from these great depths of revelation that Jesus taught, worked miracles, and inspired thousands. The greater the submission, the greater the obedience, the greater the revelation and inspiration; this is the foundation for every great, godly leader. Jesus's life and ministry were fully submitted to the Father's leading.

The next building block for a great, godly leader is connection. We see this in Jesus's life as well. He was connected to His disciples and showed genuine compassion to the crowds that followed Him. Regarding His disciples, He spent every day—all day and all night—with them. He walked with them, talked with them, ate with them, prayed with them, and worshipped God the Father with them. We see deep connections between Jesus and the twelve forged through hours upon hours of fellowship, but Jesus's connection to humanity did not stop with the twelve disciples. He also showed love and compassion to the multitudes, including those who were considered of lesser value to society in that day and age, such as women, children, and Samaritans. We see Him sparing the life of an adulteress in John 8, extending love to the littles by saying, "Let the little children alone, and do not hinder them from coming to me," in Matthew 19:14, sharing His message of love and truth with an outcast Samaritan woman in John 4, and innumerable examples of being moved with compassion and healing people physically and spiritually. Jesus's life and ministry were built upon His connection to those around Him, a connection that was generated by His heart of love and compassion (i.e., warmth).

The next building block of a great, godly leader is honesty, which we see consistently throughout Jesus's life. His words were honest, so much so, that it upset certain groups of people—namely the religious leaders. The Bible documents corruption within the religious leadership during Jesus's time on Earth, from extorting the people (see Matthew 21, Mark 12, and Luke 11) to twisting Scriptures for their own benefit (see Matthew 23). Jesus's words were full of integrity and honesty, and that was deeply disturbing to those who preferred to cloak themselves with disingenuousness. In fact, they were so disturbed that all they could think of was finding a way to get rid of Him. After all, if they silenced His voice, they could continue with their dirty work, amassing wealth and power for themselves. However, light always triumphs over darkness, and the honesty and integrity that Jesus lived mobilized and inspired those who followed Him. Even when they did silence His physical voice, His teachings and inspiration lived on in His followers—and continue to this day, perpetuated through the Holy Spirit and the written Word.

Jesus was also an authentic person. John 13:3 says, "Jesus, knowing that the Father had given all things into His hands, and that He had come forth from God and was going back to God," means that He knew exactly who He was and what His purpose was. He was the Son of God, and His words and actions demonstrated this reality to everyone around Him every moment of every day. Over the course of the Gospels, we see that He never wavered once from His mission and, as He accomplished God's plan, He maintained His integrity and authenticity to the end. Jesus was true to who He was and to God's plan for His life; Jesus's life and ministry radiated honesty, integrity, and authenticity.

The next facet of leadership that we see in Jesus's life is authority. Time and again we see the people of Jesus's day awed by His teachings, which were unlike any other they had ever heard. Why? Matthew 7:29 tells us, "He was teaching them as one who has authority, and not as their scribes." Jesus's words had a quality about them that drew people in…lots of people. I imagine He spoke with confidence and perhaps had a way of speaking that made people feel like He was talking right to them. Regardless, we see Him mobilizing crowds, casting out demons, healing the sick, and raising the dead with His words. His words were backed up by the miraculous works God did through Him because Jesus worked under the authority of God (see the above paragraph about submission).

Furthermore, we see Jesus delegating this authority to His disciples in Luke 9:1-2, "[a]nd He called the twelve together, and gave them power and authority over all the demons and to heal diseases. And He sent them out to proclaim the kingdom of God and to perform healing." Jesus gave His closest disciples the power to speak and work miracles because a good leader knows it takes more than one person to complete a mission. A leader who insists on micromanaging every single aspect of every single project usually winds up frazzled and burned out, and the project will most likely remain small, or worse, incomplete. But a good leader knows that it takes a team to achieve greatness, and trusted members of that team can, and should, be given authority.

Wise delegation is a hallmark of a good leader because it enables team members to learn and to grow which increases overall productivity and facilitates achievement. Jesus's life was marked by authority, and His ministry was exponentially increased due to wise delegation of this authority as well as by impartation of the Holy Spirit. This delegation and impartation have continued through the generations as the church continues to walk in Jesus's authority and fulfill His commission, which He gave to us in Matthew 28:18-19 when He said, "All authority has been given to me in heaven and on earth. Go therefore and make disciples of all the nations, baptizing them in the name of the Father and the Son and the Holy Spirit." Inevitably, as we accomplish this charge, new leadership will rise up to grasp the baton from those who led before them, and the delegation and impartation that began with Jesus's leadership continues.

Jesus's life and ministry epitomize positive, godly leadership, and we see the rippling results of that to this day. We see Jesus first and foremost obeying the Father, then connecting to others, treating others with love and compassion, wielding and delegating authority, and living and speaking with honesty, integrity, and authenticity. What an incredible example of gentleness in leadership! The impact of a godly, positive leader cannot be understated. If secular research shows significant team growth in the business world from a positive leader, imagine what we as the body of Christ could accomplish with God and positive godly leaders leading the way!

Challenge Questions:

1. Are there areas in my life that I need to submit to the Lord? Take some time to ponder this as you surrender these areas to Him.
2. Are my spiritual ears open to hear the Lord on a daily basis? How can I be more intentional about listening to His voice?
3. Lord permitting, how can I share His message with those around me? What steps can I take in growing my faith as it relates to sharing His messages and words with others? To whom can I be accountable to when it comes to sharing words, visions, and dreams that the Lord gives me?
4. Do I obey the leading of the Lord? If not, what steps can I take to demonstrate greater obedience to His guidance and plans?
5. How can I show greater value to others through actions consistent with God's love and compassion?

Making the Connections

Positive leadership can make such a difference, and as we've seen, the traits of warmth, honesty, and authority are important, but part of what makes a positive leader great is connection to the team. Therefore, a positive leader should also attune to the needs and vision of the team; in order to do this, a leader must listen. And not half-heartedly. Really listen.

Considering we have two ears, one would think we'd be really awesome listeners, but sadly, this just isn't the case. It is surprising how poorly people listen. Too often we're so concerned with planning what we're going to say next that we only half-listen. We do this so automatically that most of us aren't even aware that we're doing it. And the sad thing is that for most of us, half-listening *is* our best listening because our smartphones, tablets, and TVs interfere, taking our minds even further from our communication partner. In my experience, in order to achieve true, authentic listening, we have to temporarily put aside our thoughts because if we are concerned with what's coming out of our mouths next, then we're not fully concerned with what's coming out of the other person's mouth *now*. Putting down our devices and turning off the TV is also a must for authentic, active listening. With authentic, active listening, the listener is fully concerned with what is coming out of the other person's mouth and *nothing else*.

When we choose to truly listen to others, it is putting someone else first, which essentially makes it akin to an act of service, humility, and love. Philippians 2:3-4 says:

> *Do nothing from selfishness or empty conceit, but with humility of mind regard one another as more important than yourselves; do not merely look out for your personal interests, but also for the interests of others.*

72

Authentic listening is one great way to live out this verse because we are putting ourselves and our concerns aside in order to fully engage with someone else. And not just externally; we are *internally* putting someone else first.

Sometimes putting another person first on an invisible level is harder than doing so externally. After all, performing visible acts of service, while absolutely valuable and needed, can still be done while putting ourselves first in our thought life. Wrestling through the invisible realm of selfishness presents its own unique set of challenges and can require quite a bit of awareness, time, and discipline. However, the rewards that can be reaped in our relationships as well as for us on a personal level are worth every thought-trapping moment. Proverbs 2:2 says, "Make your ear attentive to wisdom, incline your heart to understanding," and Proverbs 18:15 says, "The mind of the prudent seek knowledge, the ear of the wise seek knowledge." In other words, listening is the basis for wisdom and understanding. If we don't truly empty our minds of our own preconceived notions and choose to listen to someone else's heart without bias, how can we ever truly understand each other? Otherwise, our own thoughts and emotions color every incoming message, and we run the risk of misconstruing the speaker's original intent.

But what are the risks of *not* practicing authentic listening? Proverbs is full of answers to that question. Proverbs says in 19:27, "Cease listening, my son, to discipline, and you will stray from the words of knowledge," in 18:2, "A fool does not delight in understanding, but only in revealing his own mind," and in 18:13, "He who gives an answer before he hears, it is folly and shame to him." Clearly, God is sending us the message that listening is incredibly important, and the consequences of not listening are risking an unwise lifestyle, foolishness (I interpreted this as immaturity, akin to a child making foolish choices), pride, and embarrassment.

Listening (to the right people of course) is essential to understanding and to growing; it develops our relationships, and according to Proverbs, even helps to develop *us*. Listening helps us grow in maturity; after all, it can take a lot of love, self-control, and discipline to wrangle our thoughts and tongues to show value to someone else. Furthermore, those three attributes—love, self-control, and discipline—are key to leaving immaturity and childishness behind. Authentic listening enables us to grow as individuals, connect with others, deepen our relationships, and therefore live as biblically gentle people.

As we've already seen, connection is crucial for a leader who desires to inspire the team. I'd have to say that it is impossible to connect without listening. Without listening, there's going to be limited connection occurring in conversations which increases the risk of team and/or relationship breakdown. In spite of the importance of listening to our relationships, studies show time and again we only listen approximately half, or less, of the time.[24] Why? Because authentic, active listening is difficult. It's difficult to put our own thoughts and judgments aside in order to concentrate on someone else; it's difficult to put our devices down or turn the TV off to fully devote our minds and time to someone else. True listening takes time and practice to acquire. Despite the difficulty, it is possible to become masters of this art form.

Active listening begins when we send signals to the other person that we are ready to listen.[16] For example, putting the phone away or turning it off/on silent, setting books or papers aside, and looking at the other person directly. After putting aside the external distractions, we must next put aside the internal ones which means we need to control our minds. We need to keep our minds from wandering and shut out our own thoughts; it may help to imagine putting our thoughts into a box before the conversation starts. Just don't forget to seal the box.

When the speaker begins to talk, the listener's goal, after dealing with distractions, is to understand both logically and emotionally the message being conveyed. In order to ensure this is happening, it is best if the listener restates the message back to the speaker *without judgment*.[7,16] From personal experience, I recommend doing this at regular intervals.

I'm the type of person that tends to verbally charge full-steam ahead; however, as it turned out, this created quite a problem. Every time I thought I was having a nice conversation with my husband, he wound up feeling like he just got a face full of dust. It took us a long time—okay, it took ME a long time—to realize this was happening. I didn't realize that he hadn't fully digested message A, and here I was on J! I'm sure I don't need to tell you that there was regular miscommunication going on which led to frustration for both of us. I felt like he wasn't listening to me, and he felt like that was all he was trying to do! So, we devised a simple hand signal for him to use when he felt like he needed a few moments to process. He would also take that opportunity to rephrase my message back to me. We could then hash out any discrepancies and proceed with the conversation. This simple fix saved us both a lot of headaches and hassles. In my house, active listening reduced conflict, promoted connection, and the end result was greater understanding and empathy between us.

Empathy is the ability to understand and feel what the other person feels, and it is my belief that one cannot listen actively without it.[10,16] Empathy can be positive, leading to greater understanding of each other, or negative, escalating conflicts as one person's physiological stress triggers the other, thereby amplifying each other's destructive emotions.[14] Incredible research has been done on the impact of empathy on our bodies. One study even found that when a spouse is experiencing negative emotions, their partner's physiology, namely their heart rate, actually mimics the spouse's.[23] *Their hearts actually beat in unison*! Intimate connection, such as marriage, lends itself to what I'll call *deep empathy* which is what that amazing study was able to show us. That study took something typically thought of as abstract and intangible and transcribed it into black and white numbers we can see and understand. Most of our relationships probably won't achieve that level of deep empathy, which enables our hearts to literally beat together, but that doesn't mean empathy is absent altogether.

Empathy is just part of being human. After reading through the research, it is my belief that empathy, which is driven by our auto-brain, the amygdala, is what causes us to mirror facial expressions from those around us. These are fleeting and imperceptible smiles, frowns, and furrowed brows. When we make these transient expressions, a shot of chemicals is released in our bodies. These chemicals are associated with particular emotions—happy, sad, or angry, just to name a few. Therefore, these automatic—and generally undetected—facial expressions we mimic every single day from every single person we encounter give us clues regarding other people's moods. And incredibly, we usually don't even realize it![3,8,13,17,21,22]

This just goes to show how interconnected we are as human beings. Our emotions and moods are contagious; we impact those around us just by walking by and giving them a look. I noticed a long time ago that if one person is negative, it doesn't take long for everyone else to be miserable too. After reading this, it may seem as though we are driven by physiology, destined to feel whatever emotions everyone else in the room happens to be experiencing at that particular moment. Absolutely not. We are not at the mercy of the moods we catch from those around us; we do have choices.

One way to counteract an encroaching negative mood is to simply smile. I've found that just smiling, even when I don't feel like it, makes me feel happier. Dr. Cuddy boldly states in her book *Presence* that our bodies tell our minds how we should be feeling. Have you ever heard the phrase *The body is a slave to the mind* before? Well, according to science, the reverse can also be true. So, if we want to feel happy, we should start acting like it, and eventually our emotions will catch up.[7]And the really good news is that if we do make the choice to be positive, the likelihood of kicking off a chain reaction in the people around us is high since positive moods are highly contagious. In fact, smiles are the most contagious facial expression of all.[16]

Contagious emotions are extremely pertinent to leadership, since the leader's emotions often have the greatest impact on the team and can set the tone for the entire department.[15] Remember, positive leaders tend to have positive, more productive, team members.

So, to sum it up, a positive, effective leader will connect with the group by first showing warmth. This is a crucial first step of enabling the group to open itself up to trust the leader. In order to maintain the trust of the group, the leader must also exhibit competence, humility, honesty (telling the truth, promoting integrity, and being authentic), and by actively listening to members of the group. By implementing these attributes, leaders are able to not just guide but also develop their teams. These teams then typically exhibit higher levels of confidence, creativity, and growth. Positive leaders are connected leaders, and godly leaders are leaders that are fully submitted to the Lord and lead from a place of love and humility. When operating in a manner consistent with positive, godly leadership, the empowerment that is achieved through connection fosters growth and development in others. This is what provides a key contribution to biblical gentleness.

Challenge Questions:

1. Do I find it easy or difficult to build authentic connections with those around me? What might be the cause? What can I do to improve my ability to connect with others?
2. Do I find it easy or difficult to maintain authentic connections with those around me? What might be the cause? What can I do

to improve my ability to maintain and deepen my connections with others?

3. What challenges do I face when it comes to authentic, active listening? What might be contributing factors? What steps can I take to overcome those challenges?

4. What can I do to show those around me that I am ready to listen to what they have to say?

5. What can I do to show those around me that I am listening to what they are saying?

6. How do I respond internally when someone around me is negative? What steps can I take to maintain a positive attitude in the midst of negativity?

7. What emotions do I convey to those around me on a regular basis? Why? Enlist the help of a mirror, friends, family, and coworkers if needed. What, if anything, can I do to present positive, rather than negative, emotions?

Self-Control

Coffee. Chocolate. Cookies. Ice cream. Potato chips. What do these have in common? They all give me serious self-control issues. Perhaps you can relate? But lack of self-control goes beyond the inability to stop or say no to something. What about other areas such as going to the gym, studying hard, and working diligently? Do these also require self-control? Every day we are faced with choices and challenges, and how we conduct ourselves and the decisions we make impact our lives. Sometimes this impact is small, but sometimes it's gargantuan. The ability to choose and behave wisely is strongly connected to self-control. But how does self-control impact our lives beyond the moment of temptation and decision? And what does self-control have to do with gentleness?

Imagine a beautiful, sunny day. It's perfect to get some shopping done. You leave your car parked in the parking lot and (gasp!) you leave your keys in the ignition! Oh…wait…you didn't actually need to gasp *there* because you *also* left your windows rolled all the way down. *Now* you can gasp because you walk out of the store with your bags and discover that your car is no longer in the lot. That's what living life is like without self-control and awareness.

In Proverbs 25:28 the Bible compares living a life of self-control to a city with no walls that has been broken into. Nowadays we don't build huge, fortified walls around each and every city, but we do lock our doors and windows. In that same vein, living a life of self-control safeguards us from the decisions in life that would rob us of peace and joy. I believe Dr. Roy Baumeister, a leading scientist on the subject of willpower and self-control, would agree with this statement. In his book, *Willpower*, he says that stress is reduced by avoiding bad decisions, and these bad decisions are avoided through self-control.[1] And again, science proves God's principles true.

I'm sure most of us are familiar with at least some of the deleterious effects of stress on our bodies, relationships, and psyche, but does self-control benefit us in any other ways—waistline excluded? Yes. Research has shown that people who exhibit self-control tend to have better grades, higher self-esteem, less substance abuse, better relationships, and have better emotional responses in general.[1,22]

Most of us may have noticed that when we are tired, we are more emotional. Now what about when we are hungry? What about after a stressful day at work or home? Ever notice that we tend to get snippy or, let's be real, downright nasty? This is in large part because after exercising self-control, people tend to feel things with greater intensity than they would otherwise.[1] A study was done to investigate *why*. Why do we react with greater intensity after we've been exercising self-control?

Within our brain there is a tiny area called the amygdala, and this area plays a significant role in nonverbal emotional processing. This process happens instantaneously and requires all of approximately a microsecond or so to occur. Having a sense about someone or "catching" someone's mood is in large part thanks to the amygdala (see the discussions in the prior chapter about authenticity and empathy), but the amygdala also comes into play when we experience negative emotions.[13] But getting back to the study, what these researchers found was that the amygdala had a *greater* response to *negative* emotional input *after* people had exercised self-control. They also found that there was *no difference* in reaction when the emotional input was *positive* between the group that had exercised self-control and the group that had not.[26] Taken together; this study showed a reduced ability to exercise self-control after experiencing negative emotional input. So, next time we slip in the self-control department after experiencing something negative, we can, in part, blame the amygdala.

But does the amygdala hold all the power? Are we victims of our physiology? Absolutely not. Self-control may seem impossible at times—resisting a bowl of ice cream on a hot day, romantic feelings that are a no-no, or warding off a fiery temper—but self-control *is* possible. No one is perfect, so that should not be the expectation. But what we can do is take every challenge as it comes, know that if we fall, it's right into God's grace, and is forgivable.

A lot of research has been done that shows that each time we use self-control, it's like taking money out of a bank account. The idea is that there's only so much there, so the more we use it, the less we have for the next time. While something as simple as food has been found to help replenish our internal self-control banks, other studies have shown that our personal beliefs about self-control are large contributors as well. Both of these elements have a significant impact on our ability to maintain control. Studies found that having a small snack when facing a self-control challenge enabled subjects to exercise greater self-control. Also, if someone believed that they were able to control themselves, studies showed that they, in fact, demonstrated greater self-control.[1,15] But food and theories only get us so far in the heat of the moment.

The first strategy to prevent a breakdown of self-control is often called *avoidance*, but I prefer the Bible's terminology: FLEE! In other words, if at all possible, we should not put ourselves in situations that set us up to fail. No loitering. No toe dipping. Not even meandering away. Turn around and run with all we've got—immediately.

There may be times, however, when fleeing is not an option, and exercising self-control may feel as impossible as deadlifting 1,000 pounds. But have hope! Where we lack, God abounds, and with God, all things are possible. Sometimes it's all we can do to take baby steps, and sometimes we need Him to carry us, but either way, in Him we are able move forward and continue to grow this crucial attribute in our lives.

One way to plan and take resolute steps to move forward is by establishing routines and organization. The idea is that when certain processes are automatic (such as grooming and filing paperwork), we no longer need to rely on our self-control to implement these tasks. Therefore, if we are trying to boost self-control, one strategy would be to make a list of areas in our lives that we want to improve. Start with one area. Just one. For example, eat a piece of fruit instead of dessert after a meal. Once the new routine is established, then, and only then, introduce another target. So, give it a few weeks before beginning to tackle the next area.

Another tool we can use to promote self-control in our lives is meditation. Remember how I shared that meditation helped pull me out of daily panic attacks? Brain imaging studies show that meditation decreases the amygdala's connection to the parts of our brain that control our fight-or-flight response and increases its connection to the areas that are crucial for

80

self-control and positive emotions.[1,13,19,20,21,23,24,29] In other words, by meditating, our auto-brain becomes more connected to areas of control and less connected to areas that lack conscious control.

This is so important, because the amygdala will automatically process negative emotional input. There's no logic, no conscious thought. So, if our amygdalas have a greater connection to the automatic processes (aka fight-or-flight), and we experience something negative after we exercised self-control—say, a child's temper tantrum after we just refused to gorge ourselves on chocolate—we run a much greater risk of having a meltdown of our own. Meditation helps limit this process by promoting the circuits of control and demoting the circuits of automaticity. Again, it is no wonder that God repeatedly encourages us to meditate on Him and His Word. He knows how hard self-control can be for us, especially when we mix in auto-brain, but, as usual, He has provided the tool; we just have to use it. After all, just because the amygdala functions automatically and too rapidly for our logic to corral doesn't mean it's a rogue member of our brain's anatomy. The amygdala works together with other portions of our brains, and we are able to use these connections to our advantage. God has given us meditation as a means to manage those automatic brain processes housed in the amygdala.

But what does all of this have to do with gentleness? Central to the biblical definition of gentleness is incredible power, but what happens if power of immense magnitude goes unchecked and uncontrolled? Volcanoes come to mind. So do earthquakes and tornados. While we may marvel over demonstrations of unbridled power, we are certainly *not* going to connect with them. I mean, I don't exactly want to be in the path of molten rock spewing from within the Earth's belly, and I'm certainly not going to use it as a campfire to sing "Kumbaya" with my friends. Repeatedly, we see that unbridled power from the Earth is cause for evacuations and results in mass destruction. It is the same in relationships.

We cannot approach our relationships without self-control. From the simple, every day, and underappreciated pleasantries, to restraining our tempers, to refusing to share the latest gossip, self-control is a must for relationships to thrive. This can be challenging when defenses are down, stress is high, and tensions mount. Both work and home environments are petri dishes that seem to culture variants of this concoction. Family members get in our faces, bosses breathe down our necks, and we sacrifice sleep in an attempt to get our to-do lists done…or to at least check off just a few more items. Let's face it. Life's clutches can be downright suffocating. What happens as the pressure mounts? An explosion? Seems reasonable. In the natural world, heat and pressure build up within the Earth and need to be vented— hence we have volcanoes. When similar emotional buildup occurs within us, it feels good *and right* to vent frustrations and anger in the moment to obtain a release that improves our mood. Right? Well…maybe not quite.

Growing up, I had quite a fiery temper. And as any child would, I released it in completely inappropriate ways. Throwing things, hitting, and biting come to mind. Fortunately, though, through discipline and correction, my parents were able to help me quell those impulses while I was still quite young. I thought they were gone forever. Life was good. I became known as a quiet, patient person. Then I had kids.

I was no longer quiet. I was no longer patient. My fiery temper spewed forth from the deepest recesses of my soul and shocked both my family and me. It began by venting my anger and frustration through socially appropriate verbal means (i.e., complaining to my husband and anyone else who would listen). Over time, though, those grumbles escalated into yelling, slamming doors, and an occasional not-so-gentle toss of an inanimate object. Clearly the initial step of venting my frustration and anger through "innocent" complaining did *not* improve my mood *or* temperament. I was sliding down the banister in a hurry and straight into a cauldron of fire.

Unfortunately, I am not the only one who has been lured into complaining's seductive trap. I've seen a similar pattern play over and over again in various areas, and almost always at a job site. Inevitably, someone has a complaint against somebody else for who knows what at some point, and that's all it takes. One complaint, then another and another, and all of a sudden there's a negative attitude. But it almost never stops there, the complaints spread and, with them, the negative attitudes until one day the whole place is rancid, poisoned with nonstop complaining and negativity.

Another example of the slippery slope of complaining can be found in Numbers. The book of Numbers begins approximately two years after the Israelites' mass exodus from Egypt. Imagine how Moses and the Israelites felt as they left Egypt; for the first time in hundreds of years they were free! And on top of that, God moved in a miraculous way with an immense display of His sovereign power at the Red Sea, bringing a swift and decisive victory.

But now, the sensational exodus is over, and it's two years later. It's been two years of waiting; two years of sore feet and dragging along tents, packs, children, and animals; and two years of walking toward a promise not yet fulfilled. Now, beginning in Numbers 11, the people of Israel begin to complain about their situation. Immediately the Lord was angered and punished the complainers; however, Moses interceded on the people's behalf, and the Lord relented.

Over the course of several chapters, we see evidence that the heart of the people has been poisoned by negativity and complaining, as they repeatedly complain against the Lord and Moses despite God's previous punishment. What I found interesting as I read through this story, is how Moses "prayed to the Lord" on behalf of the people in Verse 2 but, by Verse 11, Moses says, "Why have You been so hard on Your servant? And why have I not found favor in Your sight, that You have laid the burden of all this people on me?" What a change in verbiage. I can only assume that listening to the constant complaints of the people wore on Moses and eventually, Moses himself began to complain about his situation.

Both the Israelites and Moses were exactly where God placed them and were walking out His plan, yet both began to grumble and complain, and this pattern continues even when they finally reach the Promised Land. Sometimes I wonder if the Israelites had chosen faith and hope over complaining and negativity, would they have made a different decision when they arrived at the fulfillment of God's promise? Would they have chosen faith over fear and doubt...and more complaining? Perhaps God's plan was to walk them through that path in the wilderness to strengthen their faith, so when they finally reached the Promised Land, they would have grown in their faith and bravely stood on His word, thereby entering and possessing the fulfillment of His promise. I guess we'll never know this side of heaven. Regardless, once again, the Israelites complained against God, choosing negativity, fear, and doubt over His promises, and they were denied entrance into the Promised Land for forty years! Imagine how Moses must have felt in this moment.

Now they are stuck in the wilderness for 40 years with no hope of ever entering into this land they just spent years walking to. The grumbling and complaining amongst the people must have been incessant. Over the next six chapters, we see Moses struggling with the Israelites and often interceding between God and the people, as God frequently became angry with the people who just couldn't stop complaining, even though it had cost them everything. I imagine at this point, in Numbers 20, Moses was at the end of his rope with the people and their negativity. In Verse 5, the people approach Moses and say, "Why have you made us come up from Egypt, to bring us in to this wretched place? It is not a place of grain or figs or vines or pomegranates, nor is there water to drink." Moses brings their complaints to the Lord, yet again, and God tells Moses to speak to a specific rock and promises that fresh, potable water will spring forth from it.

However, when Moses stands in front of the Israelites, watch what happens in Numbers 20:10-11: He said to them, "Listen now, you rebels; shall we bring forth water for you out of this rock? Then Moses lifted up his hand and struck the rock twice with his rod..." There are two key points in these verses: one, Moses insults the people when he says, "You rebels," and two, he didn't speak to the rock, which is what he was told to do, he hit it. Moses had suffered for years leading people whose hearts were so blinded by self-focus, complaining, and negativity that they couldn't see the truth, nor could they see God's plan *even when they were told*, and in the process lost his focus on God's command and fell into disobedience. The Israelites had found ways to complain about each and every situation they were in, right down to God's miracles and provision for them, and the negativity spread throughout the entire nation.

Complaining rarely remains contained and often spreads to all who come in contact with it. It causes greater negativity and aggression and, in this passage in Numbers, we see that even Moses was affected. We see him begin by venting to God about the people and eventually spiral all the way to exhibiting aggression by insulting the people and hitting a rock. Clearly, venting did not help Moses either. And how seriously does God take this? Well, in Numbers 20:12, God tells him, "Because you have not believed Me, to treat Me as holy in the sight of the sons of Israel, therefore you shall not bring this assembly into the land which I have given them." God takes this issue *very* seriously.

So, if venting our frustration and anger doesn't actually improve our moods, then why do we do it? Simple. When we vent our frustration or anger, whether it is through something that appears innocent, such as repeated griping, or outright retaliation to someone who has wronged us, it immediately triggers the reward center of our brain.[7] This physiological validation of our choice is what lures us in. Just like everything else that opposes God's way of doing things, immediately it feels good. It may even feel right. Unfortunately, that feel-good feeling just doesn't last. In fact, that positive feeling not only goes away, it actually turns the tables on us. Studies repeatedly show that people who vent their anger or retaliate are *less* happy *longer* than those who do not.[4,5,6] But why? Why would something that seems to release the toxic potion of emotions that simmers within us in actuality amplify and prolong it? Because we continue to focus on it.

Consistently, when people focus on what made them angry, they stay angry, and their aggression can actually *increase*.[3,4,5,6,10] This focus can take the form of personal thoughts (rumination), vocal complaints, or behavioral retaliation (in any form, even if it isn't directed at the offender). And it gets worse. Being focused on what makes us angry doesn't stop there because choosing anger and aggression tends to make us gravitate toward violence, other angry people, and aggressive actions.[4,5,6,28] In other words, this focus, as innocent as it may seem, often results in a fiery, self-perpetuating spiral that is just waiting to explode.

As I read this research, my personal experience began to make sense. By allowing myself to internally focus on what made me upset, I had allowed myself the next baby step of verbal complaints. If venting alone was enough to resolve my emotional problem, it would have been fixed almost immediately. The problem was that venting didn't fix it. In actuality, that was only the first baby step toward my downfall. Once I was in its grip, it kept pulling me deeper and deeper, and before long, I didn't even recognize myself, nor did I like who I had become. I had slipped down the slope all the way to behavioral aggression. This then begs the question: if our natural inclination of rumination, venting, and possibly retaliation is incorrect and, in fact, actually harmful, then what *should* we be doing?

Much of the research promotes an initial distraction to keep our minds from doing what comes naturally—focusing on what upset us.[4,5,6] Beyond that, there is research to support expressions of gratitude, reframing the incident, praying for blessings on those that offended you, relaxation (i.e., such as meditation), and forgiveness.[3,11,17,27,30] And of course, this research affirms the truth already written in the Bible.

Philippians 4:6-7 says:

Be anxious for nothing, but in everything by prayer and supplication with thanksgiving let your requests be known to God. And the peace of God which surpasses all comprehension will guard your hearts and minds in Christ Jesus.

In other words, when we pray and express gratitude to the Lord, He promises that His peace will guard our thoughts and our emotions. Therefore, when we pray, praise, and give thanks, it helps prevent us from getting trapped by complaining and anger because when God's peace fills us, there is no room for the tumult of complaining and anger.

Furthermore, regarding prayer, Jesus Himself commands us to pray for those who come against us in Matthew 5:44. Why? Well, I believe it's two-fold. One, to release God's love and power in their life, so they may be saved and blessed, and two, for us. He knows that it is difficult for us to maintain negativity toward someone when we are actively praying for God to bless them. We may need to pray through gritted teeth sometimes, but pray we must in order to keep our hearts full of God's love, soft and pliable in His hands; otherwise, we run the risk of becoming hardened and full of anger and bitterness. Stephen was a prime example of a heart full of God's love; just before he died at the hands of his persecutors in Acts 7:60, he prayed, "Lord, do not hold this sin against them." What an incredible heart! Talk about praying blessings and choosing tough forgiveness. Through his pain, which I can only imagine was immense at that moment, he offered forgiveness and blessing. Not anger. Not resentment. No complaining either. I believe this type of heart was cultivated over years of choosing faith, forgiveness, and love over complaining, negativity, and anger.

Scriptural meditation can also help combat anger and complaining by focusing our minds on His Word. The Bible offers additional promises for us when we engage in Scriptural meditation in Psalm 1:2-3 "...in His law he meditates day and night; he will be like a tree planted firmly by streams of water, which yields its fruit in season and its leaf does not wither, and in whatever he does, he prospers." As we've already seen, complaining and anger breed negativity and destruction. Destruction to relationships and our biblical example show that when we choose to complain, we can actually block God's promise from being fulfilled in our lives. That's not growth, and it's not prosperity. However, in this verse we see that Scriptural meditation engenders growth in our lives which is evidenced to those around us, and God even promises prosperity. Sounds like promises fulfilled, not blocked.

Sounds like making the choice to engage in Scriptural meditation is a tool we can use to quell the complaints.

Reframing the offending incident can help us overcome anger and complaining as well. By reframing the incident, I mean to think about it in a new and different way. For example, much of my downward spiral was initially due to my profound disappointment and devastation that my lifelong dream of being a stay-at-home mother was never going to be a reality. Since I indulged myself in a self-pity fest, I grew resentful toward my husband (why couldn't he just *make* this happen) which opened Pandora's Box in our relationship. After I *finally* worked through my anger, I came to the conclusion that I could choose to continue to be sad and miserable, or I could choose to be content with where God has placed me, trust in His wisdom and His plan, and choose to be positive.

In order to help me maintain a more positive attitude, I reframed the offensive situation from, "How *dare* he not find a way for me to resign from my professional position," to, "I'm grateful to have a job that I enjoy and great coworkers that I look forward to see," and, "I'm glad that my children have the opportunity to spend quality time with their father without me so they can develop closer bonds." Surprise, surprise, my mood and behavior improved, and I found myself wishing that I had done this much, much sooner.

Take a moment to think about the story I just shared. Notice that my initial "offending" incident wasn't even one where I was overtly wronged by anyone, and, actually, in the beginning, I wasn't even angry. In fact, I was depressed. This brings me to a quick side note about anger: in my experience, anger often covers other emotions. In my own life, whenever I feel angry, I always spend some time soul-searching for another emotion. Maybe it's sadness, shame, or fear.[12,25] I've found, and so has the research, that these particular emotions like to hide behind anger like toddlers hide behind their parents. My opinion is that this occurs because we perceive these as "weak" emotions while anger, on the other hand, appears strong. One intriguing study even showed that there were similar neural activation patterns between anger and fear.[12] But is anger really as powerful as it appears to be? Are people really stronger when they are angry? I'd have to say it's a resounding NO.

Anger is seductive. It feels powerful. It looks powerful. It does sometimes make other people stop in their tracks, cower or cringe, and possibly do whatever we want them to do, but there's a downside. Eventually, we lose control as anger gains control over us.[2,4,5,6,9,14,16]. Unfortunately, I discovered this the hard way. Furthermore, angry people have a harder time building and maintaining social connections.[16,18] And finally, anger is hard on our bodies; it has been associated with high cholesterol, coronary heart disease, high blood pressure, and heart attacks.[8,17] It seems to me that while anger *appears* powerful, it's really a life-sucking parasite, taking our happiness, joy, vitality, and, eventually, us.

Ditching the parasite of self-centered anger in exchange for self-control is essential to living a lifestyle of gentleness. After all, as we've established, anger weakens, it does not strengthen. It weakens the person unleashing anger *and* usually harms the recipient of the anger. Furthermore, the "power" of anger is not one that, in my opinion, we are able to control, and by definition biblical gentleness is the controlled wielding of power that brings benefit and connection to others. So, the next time we feel frustration and anger beginning to build up pressure within us, remember that volcanoes aren't the only thing made by heat and pressure. Diamonds are, too. We have a choice: we can choose to be an explosive volcano and potentially destroy whatever's around us, or we can allow God to help us become a pressure-cooked diamond and share the beauty that God creates within us with all we encounter.

In conclusion, biblical gentleness encapsulates the attributes of power under control. Unbridled power has the potential to cause devastating destruction, whereas power under control can produce results limited only by the imagination. By choosing self-control, we give ourselves the opportunity to deepen connections with others and maintain harmony, which benefits both us and those around us. Additionally, we are able to experience greater emotional balance, foster positive attitudes, and promote health within our bodies and minds. Self-control promotes constructive power, and when we turn our minds to the Lord, makes diamonds.

Challenge Questions:

1. What are some situations in my life that cause negative emotions? Write down specific emotions.
2. What are my exact thoughts about the situations I wrote down for question number one? Write them down. How are my thoughts perpetuating the negative emotions?

3. How can I reframe the situation to foster positive emotions? Write down these reframed thoughts and place them in a highly visible area.

4. What Bible verse speaks to my thoughts, feelings, and/or situation from the above exercise? Write it down and place it in a highly visible area.

5. When have I felt anger? Is there another emotion hiding behind the anger? Find a Bible verse that speaks to that emotion. (If you need help processing that situation/emotion, please seek professional help.)

6. What situations in my life typically cause frustration and/or anger? What can I do to help diffuse those negative emotions without venting? Suggestions include regular meditation on the Word, practicing gratitude (regularly and in the moment), taking deep breaths, naming the emotion, finding a distraction, praying blessings over the other person, and respectfully and openly discussing your feelings with the other party.

7. When have I lost self-control? What were the feelings and choices that led up to losing self-control, and what were the consequences afterward?

8. What can I do differently in the future to prevent my behavior from question seven? What steps will I take to prevent losing self-control in the future? What can I do to mend things from past situations where I've lost control? Be specific.

9. What areas in my life do I want to improve? These can be anything from daily routines and organization to interpersonal skills. List several and then choose one. Create a specific action plan for this one behavior. After this new habit is formed, choose another area and repeat.

Kindness

A cts such as holding a door open for someone else, treating someone else to lunch, or writing an encouraging note to someone who is down seem so simple, maybe even trite. But the impact of kindness can be profound and not just for the receiver.

Kindness ripples throughout our society. Sometimes the ripples are small, and sometimes they're tsunamis. It isn't any wonder that in Old English, the word *kindness*, originally spelled *kyndnes*, meant "nation" and "to produce, increase."[15] We certainly still see those characteristics today; kindness often breeds more kindness and builds connections between people, making kindness a potent facet of gentleness. And it's not just the grandiose gestures that count; little everyday acts of kindness can pack a wallop of their own.

It all probably started with one rock. Perhaps someone just wanted to cheer up a friend and left a painted rock with a cheery face or message. Regardless of what the initial spark was, the thought of hiding a pretty rock to spread kindness and positivity sparked a movement that led to multiple Facebook groups with many thousands of members, at least one feature in the news, and thousands of rocks hidden throughout multiple counties, states, and countries. In my area, this movement was coined *Berks County Rocks* and is a prime example of what the literature calls *contagion*, or the spreading of one emotion or behavior to others. Another example of the kindness contagion is the pay-it-forward chain which starts when one person pays for the person behind them at a tollbooth or a drive-through. The chain continues, each person paying for the person behind them, until someone breaks the flow. Kindness moves many, but it often only takes one to start the wave.

Sometimes the impact of kindness is clear. A smile. A teary thank you. But are there benefits to kindness beyond what the eye can see? Beyond that smile? Beyond the tears? The warm fuzzies? What are those anyway?

Warm fuzzies. That's the very technical term used to describe the warm sensation that spontaneously erupts from our chests when we receive kindness, witness an act of kindness, or are kind to someone else. Scientists have associated that sensation with the chemical in our bodies called oxytocin, which is well known for its roles in pregnancy, lactation, and social bonding. For many years, it was believed that oxytocin was only produced in our brains, however, evidence has surfaced that the heart is another manufacturing center for this hormone. When oxytocin is released, we feel that warmth sensation because it opens up our arteries; this increases blood flow and reduces blood pressure.[14,21] Oxytocin also helps reduce inflammation, can act as an antioxidant, and regenerates muscle.[9,14] Those warm fuzzies? It turns out that they don't just feel good; they actually *are* good.

As if cardiac benefits weren't enough, kindness can actually slow down the aging process. It does this through muscle regeneration, promoting vagal tone, boosting the immune system, increasing nitric oxide levels, and improving telomere length.[2,9,10,13,31]

It's no secret that we lose strength as we age. Most of us begin to lose muscle mass after our thirtieth birthday, and the rate of loss increases decade by decade as we get older. *Sarcopenia* is the term for this progressive muscle loss related to aging and, in 2004, it was estimated that a whopping 45% of the geriatric population in the USA was impacted. If that statistic wasn't staggering enough, try this one: the hospital tab of sarcopenia-related cases was roughly $18.5 BILLION in the year 2000.[31] Obviously, the best weapon we have against this condition is maintaining a healthy diet and regular exercise, but kindness can wield a power of its own. This is because when we are kind, it causes our bodies to produce more oxytocin, as was already discussed above. Oxytocin, as it turns out, is necessary to help our bodies take our stem cells, or the undifferentiated cells in our bodies, and convert them into muscle cells—both skeletal and cardiac.[3,9,19] Kindness helps stay us strong by keeping our muscles fresh.

Vagal tone refers to the tenth cranial nerve, the Vagus Nerve. This is a very long nerve that wanders its way from the brain all the way down to the abdomen. The impact of this singular nerve on our physiology is astounding; it controls things like our voices and throats as well as our lungs and hearts. It is also associated with the parasympathetic nervous system, the system that combats the fight-or-flight response to threats and stress, and maintains the body's cycle of replenishing itself. Good vagal tone is associated with being emotionally resilient, which is the ability to adapt well to stressful situations and crises.[23] In addition, part of this nerve's duties in respect to its role with our heart and lungs is that it syncs heart rate with breathing. This synchronization then contributes to what is known as *heart rate variability*, or the measure of the variation of time between heartbeats, which is a reliable measure of cardiac health. As we age, our vagal tone tends to decrease; this leaves us more vulnerable to stress and possibly also cardiovascular disease.[1,8,17] Therefore, maintaining the excellent vagal tone we are born with is one way to combat aging, and kindness promotes vagal tone.

Growing up, I noticed that if I got a cold, I might sniffle and cough for a few days. It was annoying, but it barely slowed me down. However, if my grandma got the same cold, she would have a nasty, body-wracking cough for a month—or more. As we get older, our immune systems just don't work the way they do when we are younger. However, research has shown that even after a short amount of time, say five minutes, of feeling compassion and warmth toward others, there is a noticeable improvement in the immune system as measured by antibodies found in saliva. These antibodies, specifically those classified as salivary immunoglobulin A, are our first line of defense against upper respiratory infections and are also associated with defending against gastrointestinal and urinary tract infections. Those with higher levels of this group of antibodies tend to have fewer illnesses and diseases.[29] Kindness helps us stay healthy by boosting our immune system.

Kindness also produces gas. Not just any gas, but nitric oxide. Nitric oxide is critical to our cardiovascular health; it helps regulate blood pressure and flow by dilating our arteries which feeds and regenerates our muscles. But it doesn't stop there. Nitric oxide is also associated with digestion as well as memory and vision health. And as if that wasn't enough, it also kills bacteria, parasites, and disrupts the metabolism of tumor cells.[26] No wonder Nobel Prize winner Dr. Louis Ignarro calls it our body's own "wonder drug."[18] Nitric oxide is produced by oxytocin, which is associated with kindness.[11] In other words; kindness produces body-restoring, heart-healthy gas.

Telomeres are a microscopic part of our cells that make a world of difference to our bodies. They are found on the ends of our chromosomes, which hold our own unique genetic code, and are vital to our ability to make copies of our own DNA and to keep our chromosomes stable. Here's the problem. Telomeres naturally shorten as we age, and their shortening is associated with a host of health problems, including cardiovascular disease.[2,10,30] Since this is obviously a natural, biological process, there's nothing we can do about it, right? To stop it completely, no, but there are some things we can do to prolong our cellular health. One way to help keep our telomeres long is by being kind.[4,14] Dr. David Hamilton, a leading researcher on the attribute of kindness, discusses kindness' effect on aging in his book, *The Five Side Effects of Kindness*, in which he writes about the impact of stress on our telomeres and how stress shortens our telomeres. Kindness, however, combats stress, and he hypothesizes in his book that one way that kindness combats aging is by reducing stress and its negative effects.[13] Kindness, the free anti-aging serum. Apply liberally and often.

Kindness has been shown to have a clear, positive impact on our bodies. But what about our minds? Our relationships?

The brain. Isn't that where it all starts? Our minds make the decision to show kindness to someone else and then our brains order our limbs, fingers, and feet to act. We've already established that when we demonstrate kindness, our brains and hearts release oxytocin which has been implicated for a long time with developing social connections by facilitating trust. [16,24] Perhaps this is one way that oxytocin fosters bonding, for trust promotes social bonding, and without trust, how can we begin to become vulnerable to someone? Kindness encourages trust and empathy which then promotes social bonding.

Kindness also fosters a positive frame of mind. Studies have shown that just thinking (i.e., meditating) about kindness to others reduces burnout and promotes emotional wellness, and in one fascinating study, meditation itself was found to promote kindness.[5,6,32] Showing affection to others also promotes healthy patterns of cortisol management, the primary stress hormone, as well as lower heart rates and cortisol levels in response to stress.[12,13] But it isn't just through reducing stress that we see the power of kindness in our minds. Demonstrating compassion was shown to improve positive feelings (aka happiness) in people aged 17-72.[25] Worried that it didn't cover the entire lifespan? Worry no longer; positive impacts of kindness have been seen in young children as well. One study looked at preschoolers and found that those who had kind friends had more positive emotions and behaviors than those who did not.[11] And unbelievably, the rippling of kindness can impact children even younger than preschool. Another study looked at children who were shown pictures of dolls. The dolls were set up to either face each other, for the purpose of promoting thoughts of positive social connection, or to face away from each other, to determine whether the visual nudging worked. The experimenter then pretended to drop a handful of sticks and watched to see what the children would do. Those who had seen the dolls facing each other were about 40% more likely to help compared to any other condition. How old were these children? Eighteen months.[27]

Kindness is highly contagious across the lifespan. What's amazing is that it doesn't matter how often it is wielded—it never loses strength. Instead, it *gains* power—power and connection, both of which are critical components of gentleness and are propagated by kindness. Kindness can make people of all ages feel happy, reduce stress, and promote health in our bodies. Kindness. It's a good thing it's contagious.

Not only can kindness spread and benefit our health and relationships, but according to the Bible, kindness can actually effect change in our lives. The Greek word used most often in the New Testament for kindness is *chréstotés* and is the noun derivative of *chréstos*. This word, however, should not be confused with the other word translated as "kind/kindness," *philanthrópia*, which means "love for mankind," "kindness," and "benevolence."[28] All of the above secular research on kindness refers to philanthrópia kindness not chréstotés kindness. Both are admirable traits, but only one comes straight from the Lord and has the power to produce undeniably positive and lasting change.[7,20]

It is the chréstos word family that is used in Romans 2:4 where Paul writes, "The kindness of God leads you to repentance." Now wait…isn't repentance that dreaded, horrible feeling we get when we do something wrong? Isn't it that all-too-humbling moment that we apologize or openly share how human we are? Absolutely not. Yes, our conscience should sting us when we do something wrong. Yes, we need to apologize to whomever we wrong or when we damage something. Yes, we should be transparent and accountable for our actions. But that isn't repentance—at least, not according to the Bible. The word used for repentance in Romans 2:4 means "a change of mind" or "a change of the inner man."[22] Therefore, God's kindness does not cause us to humbly share our sins or apologize; it is so much more than that. It is the catalyst for us to change on a fundamental level.

I vividly remember a corporate prayer vigil I attended one year because some friends had been invited to provide music for it. My friend graciously extended his invitation to me, and I got a slot in the event. Right before it was my turn to take the mic, the moderator spent a lengthy amount of time talking. As she spoke, the atmosphere in the room went from light, lively, and joyous to heavy, dark, and sad. Why? Her speech was about how we are full of sin and the only way to change our evil ways is to focus on how awful we are and divulge this to everyone around us.

As she spoke, I remember thinking that the Bible doesn't tell us that focusing on our imperfections causes repentance; the impetus is God's kindness. It's His acts of love, rooted in His goodness, that are the key to unlocking the change and therefore the potential in our lives. So when it was my turn to take the mic, I encouraged the group to focus on God's kindness and love toward us and allow His presence to reach into their hearts. Jesus didn't die so we could focus on ourselves and our shortcomings; He suffered and died so we could be free and unified with Him. Rejoice and live in it!

When we focus on ourselves and our shortcomings, we are like a sputtering car engine, there's a whole lot of huffing and puffing but no movement. Instead, we need to shift our focus to Him and celebrate His gift of salvation, His act of kindness toward us, and *that* is what changes us. It's our continual focus on Him and His kindness that perpetuates ongoing change in our lives and constantly guides us away from our sin nature—and *that* is living a life of true biblical repentance. He has done and will do all the heavy lifting; all we need to do is focus our minds on Him, follow His lead one step at a time, and believe in Him. Don't sputter. We can let the effort be God's as we continually move toward Him in our lives by obeying His leading and His Word.

What happened at that prayer vigil? After I encouraged the group, I shared my song. The focus shifted from our sinful, imperfect selves to God's love, the presence of the Lord filled the room, and people were visibly touched by Him. The atmosphere changed. Heaviness became sweetness.

That's the power of God's kindness.

How does God's kindness differ from our kindness? Why is it turbocharged? As already mentioned, the word used for God's kindness is chréstotés; there is no word in the English language that is equivalent to chréstotés. According to HELPS word studies, this word is a mixture of the traits good and kind and encapsulates the concept of a goodness that is produced through the Holy Spirit that meets someone's needs in just the right way and at just the right time.[7] This is why God's kindness is able to change someone. It isn't just a deed that can pep us up momentarily (which does have value!); it goes deeper than that. It's like an invasion of perfect goodness in someone's life right when they need it and in exactly the way they need it. It's a deluge of hope that gives someone a lifeline, lights the path to change, and gives them the strength to get there. I imagine that at that prayer vigil, God was ministering to each person's heart in a unique way as they focused on His love, and He inundated them with His love and hope. No wonder focusing on His kindness enables us to have a soul makeover.

God showed me a long time ago that what we choose to focus our minds on, we will eventually become. But don't take my word for it, take His. Proverbs 23:7 says, "As a man thinks in his heart, so he is." Therefore, if we input violence, we become more aggressive. If we indulge in unforgiveness, we become bitter. But if we input love and kindness, we become more joyous, gracious, and kind. That's why He did *not* say to focus on our wrongdoings to improve our lives because the only action we'll wind up taking is circles around our own wrongdoings. What He *did* say in Philippians 4:8 was to focus on what is true, right, praiseworthy, lovely, honorable, and pure. Why? Because that's how we move toward the goal of possessing those attributes, and I can't think of a better description for God's kindness than Paul's list in Philippians 4:8— true, right, praiseworthy, lovely, honorable, and pure.

God admonishes His people over and over again to remember what He did for them and to tell others. What other purpose would this have than to instill faith, hope, and progressive change away from our sin through His powerful kindness? What we allow to reside in our minds and hearts will come out of our mouths and show in our actions. Don't believe me? Let's take a look at Luke 6:45 where Jesus is teaching the masses and says, "The good man out of the good treasure of his heart brings forth what is good; and the evil man out of the evil treasure brings forth what is evil; for his mouth speaks from that which fills his heart." James 3 also talks at length about the impact our words have on our lives and likens our words to the rudder that steers a boat or a bit in the mouth of a horse. Taken together, what is in our hearts comes out our mouths and has the ability to directly impact our lives.

No wonder God commands us to take "every thought captive to the obedience of Christ" in 2 Corinthians 10:5. Furthermore, Romans 12:2 tells us to "be transformed by the renewing of [our] mind[s]." In other words, God's formula for our metamorphosis to holiness starts with our thought lives—that capture and renew through His power. But God's love is so great; He didn't stop with just telling us this formula to change. He also promised that He would provide the way—His kindness. His chréstotés kindness that is the perfect key to unlock whatever is keeping us down, if we let it. His chréstotés kindness floods our lives with His goodness, shows us how to change, lifts us up, and helps us get there. His kindness is the secret to our transformation from the inside out. And what's more, His kindness doesn't cost us a thing.

God literally gave us for *free* everything we need to become more than what we could become on our own. The tools are not difficult to find or wield. The tools are simple. Accept God's gift of love through Jesus and then allow His Spirit to work in us. God has provided the recipe, the tools, and the elbow grease. All we have to do is use them, and when we do, He promises to change our lives.

What I found even more incredible is that this amazing, life-changing gentle kindness isn't reserved for God's use alone. It is the chréstos, not philanthrópia, word family used for the word kindness in Galatians 5:22 "but the fruit of the Spirit is…kindness." This means that as we allow Him to change us, we too are able to possess this attribute in our lives. We too are able, through God's power, to reach into someone else's life, demonstrate powerful goodness, and effect change. Do, however, please note that this kindness is a spiritual fruit, not a gift. Both gifts and fruit of the Spirit are powerful. Both are directly from God. Both can and should be shared with those around us, but there are two distinct differences. Gifts are given; fruit is grown. Growing God's fruit requires intimacy with the Lord, dependency upon Him, and our consistent participation in God's works in our lives over time.

So, let's begin to focus on God's kindness rather than our imperfections, abilities, or even accomplishments. Perhaps we can focus on the wonderful things He's done in our lives, or we can choose passages from the Bible. Let's focus our thoughts on Him and allow Him to change our lives in ways we can't even imagine. Let's abide in God's kindness and in so doing, walk in true, life-changing repentance.

Kindness is contagious and powerful. It promotes social bonding and connection along with life-changing growth and change. Without kindness, it would be difficult to foster the type of connection and trust that is essential to biblical gentleness. Without kindness it would be difficult, if not impossible, to nurture another into maturity, to facilitate mental, emotional, and spiritual healing, and support growth in others. Without kindness it would be difficult to avoid harshness. These qualities make kindness a vital ingredient to gentleness.

Challenge Questions:

1. How often do I do an act of kindness for someone else?
2. What, if any, barriers do I face in completing acts of kindness? How can I overcome these?
3. What are some acts of kindness I can do for others every day? Think of specific people and specific acts. These don't have to be big!
4. What thoughts dominate my mind on a daily basis? (Be honest and take a few days to journal if you need to.)
5. Do any of my thoughts from #4 fail to align with Scripture? Which ones? Take some time to research the Bible if needed.
6. What Bible verses specifically speak to or address my misaligned thoughts?
7. How has God shown His love to me? Be specific.
8. List at least three Bible verses that speak of God's love toward me.
9. Have I resisted God's change in my life? If so, in what areas? What can I do differently to allow God to work in my life?
10. Have I resisted God's nudges to reach out to someone else? What can I do differently so I can be used to show God's power and love to those around me?

Humility

H umility is one of those traits that is often misunderstood. So many times it is viewed, consciously or subconsciously, in the same category as timidity. Humility, however, is anything but timid. Humility is crucial to enabling us to be powerful, effective ministers of the Lord which makes it yet another indispensable component of gentleness.

Simply put, humility involves seeing ourselves the way God sees us and then turning the same kind, gentle focus onto others. Sounds easy. And it would be easy except our natural human inclination is to have distorted self-perceptions (positive or negative) and to look out for ourselves first. So…we naturally focus on ourselves. Logic says that the recipient of our focus should improve; therefore, if we focus on ourselves, we should make ourselves better. However, when we focus on ourselves and our wants and needs, we tend to create distorted perceptions of ourselves and the world at large. Furthermore, as Christians, we know that biblical wisdom almost *never* correlates with worldly wisdom. If anything, it's generally the opposite. But just in case, let's explore potential outcomes of out-of-balance self-focus.

Scenario number one. A young girl watches from the sidelines as groups of people mix and mingle, laughing, joking, and playing. She longs to join but can't. Why? She's so focused on her imperfections and worried that others will notice them too. So, rather than attempting the simple gesture of joining in with peers, this girl stands all alone, watching, wishing, and hoping someone would extend an invitation. Each passing moment, she becomes more and more aware of how she is different—maybe even inferior—compared to her peers. This self-focus did not generate boldness. It did not forge relationships. If anything, she ended up missing out on connecting with others and creating new friendships.

Scenario number two. A teen begins to become aware of how he appears different from others. He becomes overly critical and harsh in regard to his appearance. He desperately tries to change his appearance so he will fit the mold of what he believes society dictates. It's so effortless for everyone else but, unfortunately, it isn't so easy for him. Nothing seems to work and perfection remains elusive. He continues to scrutinize every single aspect of himself, from the outside in, wondering how everything comes so easily for the rest of the world. This self-focus did not result in improvement, nor did it bring him closer to anyone else. In this case, he became depressed and isolated over his inability to successfully mold himself into what society demands.

Scenario number three. A young woman feels wronged. Instead of choosing to forgive, she nurses her injured feelings which makes her incapable of mentally and emotionally moving past the hurtful actions. Thoughts like, *How could he/she do that to me, I would never do that to him/her,* and *I deserve better* fill her mind. By continuing to zoom in on the source of the hurt, she continues to focus on herself, her feelings, and her pain, rather than including the perspectives of others. The initial and continual choice of unforgiveness leads her down a path of resentment, bitterness, and eventually anger, which simmers in her heart. The anger constantly percolates and singes those around her as recompense for the slightest infraction. In this case, instead of imploding into depression, inappropriate self-focus caused her to explode in anger and alienate those around her.

Scenario number four. A man notices that he does something well. He rejoices and delights in the praise and attention he receives. He begins to focus on all the things he does well and eventually, slowly, comes to believe he does everything better than everyone else. He then refuses to delegate or accept help and begins to speak condescendingly to those around him. After all, he's better than they are anyway, or so he thinks. In this final case, self-focus did not result in collaboration or unity; it resulted in pride, conceit, self-importance, and isolation.

There is one common ending to all four scenarios above. Isolation. Most of us are at least somewhat familiar with at least one or more of these paths, whether we have trekked down them ourselves or have noticed someone close to us doing so. I personally know the first three paths well; those scenarios were ones I have lived over and over again. Regardless of which path is taken, consistent and inappropriate self-focus does not lead to the unity and fellowship that God calls us to in the Bible. It leads to isolation by means of conceit, anger, depression, timidity, or some combination thereof.

What did God say after He created Adam? In Genesis 2:18, He says, "It is not good for [people] to be alone." He created us to need relationships—with Him and with each other. However, our sinful, self-focused nature seeks to steal the fulfillment of that fundamental need from us; even if it is completely convinced it is doing otherwise. Without healthy relationships we can implode or explode and are rendered ineffective. The best tool to accomplish this is self-focus. Why? It's easy and requires no one else.

What makes the problem of self-focus even more complicated is that we *do* need some focus on ourselves or else we fall apart. For example, without getting proper rest, our brains won't function as well, and without proper nourishment, our bodies get sick more easily among other potential hazards. Therefore, clearly, we need to pay some attention to ourselves and what we need. Unfortunately, it is easy to slip and slide from appropriate to inappropriate focus; this can begin externally or internally. It can also begin innocently, perhaps even justifiably; but inappropriate self-focus has gaping pitfalls at the end of each and every path. Fortunately, God has the answer—humility, an integral part of true kindness and, in turn, gentleness.

As I said in the beginning of this chapter, one aspect of humility is seeing ourselves as God sees us because this enables us to have accurate self-focus. This is of utmost importance because without seeing ourselves correctly, we run the risk of falling into the comparison trap. Without beginning with the confidence and security of understanding our position in the Lord and our identity in Christ, our human nature can rear its ugly head and threaten to warp our self-perception. If our self-perception gets warped, our focus on others may be rooted in selfishness, pride, or fear rather than love, confidence, and God-sourced power. Therefore, an accurate, Christ-centered self-identity is the basic foundation of humility.

Jesus Himself modeled this at the Last Supper in John 13:3-5:

> *Jesus, knowing that the Father had given all things into His hands, and that He had come forth from God and was going back to God, got up from supper, laid aside His garments, and taking a towel, He girded Himself. Then He poured water into the basin and began to wash the disciples' feet.*

Notice some key points in this passage: Jesus, before focusing on His disciples and demonstrating an act of love and service toward them, knew exactly who He was in the Father. Yes, we previously discussed this exact passage as being an example of authenticity. But recognizing our position relative to God, and then acting upon the knowledge of who we are in Him, is both authenticity and the foundation for humility. Therefore, Jesus, knowing who He was in the Father (humility) also acted upon and in line with that knowledge (authenticity). This passage is thus a prime example for both attributes. But getting back to the discussion at hand—humility.

Jesus did not wash His disciples' feet out of pride and selfishness ("Hey! Look at what an amazing act of service I'm doing! I'm awesome!") or out of fear ("Oh, I hope they like me now, and I fit in."), He washed His disciples' feet knowing He was the Son of God, what God's plan for His life was, and knew that all His validation was in the Father. He didn't need any praise or reciprocation from anyone; He did this act, an ultimate demonstration of humility, for one reason: to show pure love. No expectations. No accolades. Simply love—which brings us to our second point.

Once the foundation of confidence in our identity in Christ is laid, we are able to properly act upon the second facet of humility, which is focusing on others. The Bible has a total of nineteen different Hebrew and Greek words that translate as "humility" or some other word in that family, such as "humble," and almost all of them contain the idea of "low" whether it's bowing, being afflicted, or low in spirit or social position.[11,12] As I was preparing to write this chapter, I wrote down all the definitions of biblical humility on a piece of paper. I read and reread and pondered. Then it dawned on me—servanthood. Of course!

All the biblical words for humility point to concepts contained in servitude. Traditionally, servants are perceived to have lower social standing and are often depicted in physically submissive, or low, postures. And despite distasteful connotations, what do sincere servants do but focus on others and put others' needs before their own? Is it any wonder why Jesus would call us to be servants? Is it any wonder that Jesus gave us a beautiful model of servanthood at the Last Supper? As someone raised in a Christian home, this concept of leading and living as a servant was taught until it became second nature. However, at the time that Jesus spoke these words, they were shocking. Maybe even revolutionary. I can hear his disciples' thoughts now:

Gentleness: It's Not What You Think

He wants me to be what?! A servant?! NO WAY!

The idea of voluntarily living as a servant contradicts our nature because by nature, we want to acquire status and power. We want attention because of how wonderful we are. We want more than a cursory glance, if that, when we're being told to do something. Yet that is the highest calling that God has for us—to be servants, and in that calling and position, we achieve greatness. Again, biblical principles that fly in the face of worldly wisdom and make us the best we can be.

As we've already seen, inappropriate self-focus does not yield the results we strive for. It does not bring us together with God or others, enable us to be effective ministers for God, or help us become resilient. It locks us up within the prison in our own minds, and the worst part is that in this prison, we are our own wardens. And we are often the WORST wardens. We can be harsh, unrelenting, and even downright brutal. And the more we focus on ourselves, the stronger the bonds of captivity become. What a vicious cycle!

God doesn't want us to be trapped in that downward spiral. He wants us to live in freedom and the way to do that is by choosing humility. By choosing to have our identity rooted in Christ. By choosing to uplift others. By choosing to be a servant. When we decide to live a lifestyle of genuine servanthood, demonstrating love toward others with no expectation of reciprocation, we are choosing a lifestyle of humility, and this is the greatest secret to freedom. By choosing biblical humility, we escape the self-inflicted prison within our own minds and are able to more clearly see opportunities to extend God's love to others, thus creating more opportunities to operate in servanthood. And the cycle continues.

When we serve others, we uplift and appreciate them. This gentle kindness forges and deepens relationships and enables the body of Christ to be the body of Christ. Otherwise, we would be as dysfunctional as Paul describes in his letter to the church in Corinth, each of us jealous and fighting with each other over the way God made and called each of us (see 1 Corinthians 6 and 1 Corinthians 11:17-31). That's no way to live! Choosing self-centeredness and refusing to collaborate gets everyone nowhere fast. No society, church, company, family, or group of friends can fully operate in that way. Gentle, kind humility opens up the path to endless possibilities, and I believe that is why Jesus tells us in Matthew 20:26-27 that in order to be great, we must be a servant. Is it easy? No way! In fact, I'd say this is so difficult, it's impossible without Jesus. In order to achieve this level of humility, we *must* be centered on Christ.

Without a Christ-centered servanthood mindset, our eyes are too focused on ourselves to see opportunities to love those around us. It is walking in God's selfless love that truly empowers believers by opening our eyes and providing unction to take action to minister to others. I'd even go so far as to say that without humility it is impossible to truly love. The beautiful definition of love found in 1 Corinthians 13 lists several attributes of love that are directly connected to humility; namely, it is not jealous, does not brag, is not arrogant, and does not seek its own. Furthermore, without humility, it becomes more difficult to forgive, be patient, be understanding, and show kindness; this is because self-focus negates the authentic expression of these characteristics. When looking at the definition of biblical love in 1 Corinthians 13, it is clear that love cannot be directed at itself; true love *must* have another as its recipient. We cannot truly love without humility.

As mentioned previously in this chapter, nearly all of the biblical definitions of humility contain some reference to position, and true humility stems from accurately perceiving the position we have in relationship first to God and then to others. According to HELPS word study, one Greek word translated as "humility," *tapeinophrosune*, is obtained when we depend on the Lord, compare ourselves to the Lord, *not others*, and is a trait that is regulated within oneself.[8] This is the word Paul used in Ephesians 4:2 when he wrote, "With all humility and gentleness, with patience, showing tolerance for one another in love," and Philippians 2:3, "Do nothing from selfishness or empty conceit, but with humility of mind regard one another as more important than yourselves." By using this word, tapeinophrosune, Paul was saying that we are not able to properly regard others without first seeing ourselves correctly in relationship to the Lord. Furthermore, these passages are commands, therefore, God is telling us that this is how we are to live.

By choosing to focus on the Lord and comparing ourselves with Him, His revelations explode in our souls, help mold our behavior and attitudes, and bring them into alignment with His. This is a great first step for an inside-to-outside method of cultivating a humble attitude: focus on the Lord and allow the revelations of who He is shape us and our attitudes to become more like the Him.

Another Greek word translated as "humility" is *prautés*, which we discussed earlier in this book. This word begins with God's inspiration and evokes great power which is controlled. There is nothing weak or timid about this word. This word shouts POWER. Also recall that the only power that is truly powerful is controlled power. Unbridled power is destructive, controlled power is effective. Prautés speaks of our position in the Lord, since the power and inspiration are His, and it also speaks of our position relative to others, since this power is then controlled and used to minister to others' hearts.[7] Therefore, biblical humility begins by recognizing our position in the Lord, and from that position, allowing His power to work through us to touch those around us.

One thing I noticed as I was researching the biblical definitions of humility is that most of them are not passive; they require a choice and a conscious effort. Moreover, Colossians 3:12 says, "put on a heart of...humility," and 1 Peter 5:5 says, "All of you, clothe yourselves with humility toward one another, for God is opposed to the proud but gives grace to the humble." In these verses we are told to put humility on. Like clothing. Just like we put on clothing each and every day, we should be choosing to be covered in a humble attitude. We should be choosing to focus on others and seeing ourselves in God's light. It protects us, allows His grace to cover us, and shows others His presence in our lives.

How does it show His presence in our lives? It does this because humility itself is divine; it's not our natural trappings. But as we make this choice every single day it becomes easier and easier to put on. Will it ever become our natural covering during our time on Earth? No, but it *can* become second nature to the point where we don't want to live without it. I mean, I certainly don't want to be caught *au naturel!* I personally prefer to put on my garments and have others see me in my garments. Just like humility. As we practice a lifestyle of humility, we come to prefer humility and prefer that others see us as humble.

As already established, living a lifestyle of true humility enables us to connect with others. Without humility, we isolate ourselves, internally and/or externally. If we are humble, not only are we seeing ourselves in a proper position relative to God, but we are also able to see others the way God sees them. When we see others the way God does, we are more apt to treat them the way He does. In other words, we are more likely to forgive, extend grace and kindness, to encourage, be patient, and to serve. When we behave in this way, it opens up the blessings of God in our lives. Is it any wonder that the Bible says in 1 Peter 5:5 that the humble will receive God's grace? What an amazing promise from God's Word! God promises undeserved blessings as a result of living a lifestyle of humility.

Godly principles result in God's blessings, but what about scientific principles? Has science shown any natural, measurable benefits of humility? To answer these questions, we'll begin on an intrapersonal level, how humility benefits the humble person, and then move on to how humility benefits our interpersonal relationships.

One surprising study from the National University of Singapore found that humility increases an individual's self-control. These researchers simply had people conjure up humble memories and found that afterwards they were able to resist chocolate longer, complete a hand grip task longer, and exhibited less frustration and more perseverance during a challenging task.[9] Another study led by Dr. Elliott Kruse from Princeton University showed that humility and gratitude worked together in tandem and predicted each other. In other words, after writing a letter of gratitude, people were humbler, and people who were considered to be humbler by nature tended to experience more gratitude.[4] It appears to be impossible to maintain self-importance while expressing thanks. No wonder God encourages us to give thanks in all circumstances in 1 Thessalonians 5:18. Humility, therefore, is a safeguard for us as individuals, but how does it impact our relationships?

One series of studies led by social psychologist Dr. Daryl VanTongeren, found that those who were humble were more accepting of others that held religious views that were different from their own, and they exhibited less aggressive behaviors toward others.[10] Another study done by a team from the University of Northern Colorado took a look at how humility impacts personal relationships, and humility was found to have a direct benefit on the quality of interpersonal relationships as measured by self-reported relationship satisfaction questionnaires.[6]

A group of researchers from the University of North Texas decided to explore the impact of humility on committed romantic relationships. They found that perceived humility (i.e., how one partner perceived the other's level of humility) was positively correlated with relationship satisfaction. Furthermore, it was directly associated with enduring and genuine commitment. This same study found that perceived humility was also correlated with forgiveness in relationships. Taken together, the researchers concluded that humility has a significant, direct and positive impact on the quality of committed romantic relationships.[2] It appears that humility improves, protects, and strengthens our relationships, too. No wonder it's an element of gentleness!

But getting back to the research. So far, science has shown that humility has a positive impact between strangers and in intimate relationships. But what about the workplace, a place where power, skills, and achievements are often rewarded with bonuses, promotions, and wage increases? The answer is a resounding, "Yes." Yes, humility benefits the workplace as well. One study led by Megan Johnson Shen from Weill Cornell Medical College examined workers who had caregiver roles and showed that Honesty-Humility was strongly, uniquely, and directly responsible for more favorable job performance ratings by their supervisors.[3] But humility doesn't only benefit those in subordinate roles. Rather, since humility by definition looks to edify and support others, companies with humble leadership tend to flourish, and the impact of humble leadership can last for decades. Humble leadership coupled with grit is positive leadership that enables growth, development, and strength within departments and entire companies.[1,5]

Bottom line: humility is necessary. It safeguards our attitudes and our relationships. It brings us together and makes us better together. Humility is not a weakness; it is power's best kept secret. Understanding our position relative to God and others empowers us to live a life of connection, change, and love. To live a life of gentleness, put on the cloak of humility every day.

Challenge Questions:

1. How often do I use or think the words "I," "me," "my," and "mine?" How often do I dominate my own thoughts? How often are these thoughts centered on my own wants/needs rather than someone else's? After completing this self-assessment, move on. DO NOT MAKE THIS A DAILY TASK.

2. Ask for feedback from those you trust and with whom you spend time regarding how humble they perceive you to be. Suggestions include your spouse, children, friends, and coworkers. Getting input from others can be difficult but is invaluable to personal growth.

3. What are my thoughts and words as they pertain to other people? Are they critical and focused on their flaws and faults? Do I look to see how I am better than they are? How can I replace negative thoughts toward someone else with positive ones? Suggestion: get to know the person, if possible. Or, if it's an entire group, learn more about that particular demographic and find your similarities and show respect for their differences. Find and appreciate their strengths and what makes them unique.

4. Do I find myself inserting myself into conversations that do not concern me? Do I participate in the daily gossip at the water cooler or over a cup of coffee? (Avoiding gossip goes a long way toward cultivating humility.) Do I involve myself in others' arguments? Do I always have to have the last word?

5. Do I dominate conversations, or do I listen to others? How often do I talk about myself and my achievements?

6. Do I encourage others? Do I use the gifts God has given me to benefit myself, others, or no one? Do I serve and strengthen those around me, or do I only invest in myself?

7. Do I take credit for what God has given me, or do I acknowledge that I am only able to accomplish through Him? Am I spending time each day praising Him and meditating on Scripture?

8. When I need help, do I ask for it, or do I bumble my way through the task? Do I accept help when it is offered? Why or why not?

9. How can I recognize others' strengths and talents? Come up with a plan to recognize or encourage one person a day. It can be simple or grandiose.

10. When I encounter a challenging situation, how do I feel? Overwhelmed? Angry? Do I persevere despite my feelings? Do I take time to pause and ask God to show me His perspective on my circumstances?

11. How can I choose to see the positive in challenges in life? How can I approach them with thankfulness rather than frustration? Can I find humor or lessons in obstacles? How can I use challenges and setbacks to improve and make myself and others

stronger? Think of one recent challenge and practice choosing optimism over obstacles.

12. When others talk to me, am I lost in my own thoughts? Am I focusing on what I want to say next? How can I set aside my thoughts so I can really listen to someone else's? What strategies can I use to be fully present in my next conversation?

13. Am I aware of how amazing life is? Am I taking the time to simply be in awe of God's design of the Earth and His unfolding plan? Am I enjoying each moment as it comes without jumping ahead to the next one? Be specific.

14. What can I be thankful for today? For this cultivation challenge, being specific is key and more is better. As special or even ordinary moments come, big or small, spend time savoring them. Do this daily.

Grace

As someone raised in a Christian household, I always associated the word grace with salvation. And, I'm sad to say, until I researched for this chapter, I rarely thought about any other purpose or reason for grace. And I certainly never connected it with gentleness. However, I have now come to appreciate that salvation is just the beginning when it comes to God's grace in our lives.

Let's begin by defining grace. According to *Merriam-Webster's* multiple entries, grace is "unmerited, divine assistance given to humans for their regeneration or sanctification; a virtue coming from God; a state of sanctification enjoyed through divine assistance," "approval, favor," "an act or instance of kindness, courtesy, or clemency," "a charming or attractive trait or characteristic," and "to confer dignity or honor on."[12] Wow! Clearly, there are many layers found in the definition of grace, and here, I had only thought of it as being defined as God's unmerited favor. But what is favor exactly? According to *Merriam-Webster's*, favor is "friendly regard shown toward another, approving consideration or attention, partiality, popularity, and assistance."[10] Taken together, according to the dictionary, grace imparts dignity and honor and extends kindness, approval, and mercy. It's unearned, undeserved, and glaringly partial toward the recipient. No wonder it's charming.[7]

But what does this mean for us in our everyday lives? Our omnipotent, holy God has approved us through His Son, in spite of our shortcomings and despite our sin; He has taken us, who deserve no honor in and of ourselves by nature, since we've created nothing in this universe on our own, and He has given us honor anyway. The implications for salvation are huge. He has elevated our status from being a mere human, drowning in our own sinful nature and imperfect choices, and through our acceptance of His sacrifice, He has given us His righteousness, a new nature, and a position in His family. He reached out to us *for the purpose of blessing us* and never ceases to do so![6,15] But it doesn't end there.

2 Peter 3:18 says, "...grow in the grace and knowledge of our Lord and Savior Jesus Christ," meaning that salvation through grace is just the starting point. Grace is what enables us to grow, and nurturing growth is a defining characteristic of biblical gentleness. The Greek word used for "in" in this verse is transliterated as *en* which is a preposition that means "within," "in the realm or sphere of," and "the condition in which something works from the inside." This word is often used when referencing a period of time (ex. *in the times of Herod*) or pregnancy (ex. she was found *to be with child*).[9]

Using pregnancy as an analogy, we are in grace as a baby is in its mother's womb. God's grace is what gives us our sustenance, strength, abilities, and develops us into who we are as His children. Without God's constant grace in our lives, we can never really change, grow, or mature. We *need* God's constant grace in order to develop past spiritual embryos. His grace surrounds us, protects us, and provides the perfect environment to produce change in us. I'll say it again—salvation is not the end of grace's role in our lives, it is only the beginning.

Grace is a source of abundant spiritual power, which is, of course, one ingredient of gentleness. 2 Corinthians 12:9 says, "My grace is sufficient for you, for my power is perfected in weakness." Without His grace in our lives, His power would not be able to flow through us. In our humanity, we would be found to be insufficient conduits for His power. His power would then blow a spiritual fuse in our lives, short-circuiting before it could ever be expressed and experienced. His grace enables us to walk in His power.

I'll never forget my senior year of high school. I was raised in a Christian home, went to church and Bible study weekly, was involved in a traveling praise band, worked at a Christian-owned restaurant, and hung out at a Christian coffeehouse. Needless to say, I was Christian Bubble Girl. As I prayed about where to go to college, the Lord laid a secular university on my heart. I applied, was accepted, and even earned a merit scholarship. All was well in the world. Then the reality of the impending bubble exodus hit me, I was terrified that I would be one of those students who left home and their faith. I sought the Lord, and His answer was so piercing that it literally still penetrates my soul to this day.

He spoke to me in a dream. In my dream, I was at the foot of a mountain that was insurmountable and impossible to climb. I knew I had to get to the other side, but I had no way to do so. I was completely overwhelmed and distressed and, in my dream, cried out, "I can't!" In that moment, He lifted me up and placed me on top of the mountain, and my entire perspective changed. In an instant. What once seemed impossible was now simple. Had I really just cried out, saying, "I can't!" a moment ago? The feeling of inability had completely vanished. I could do this. This mountain had nothing on me. Actually, now that I had a better view of it, it was really more of a large rock than a mountain. Then He spoke, "It's not about your ability to climb whatever mountains you come across in your life; it's about My grace being more than enough to conquer any mountain you may ever face."

That's the power of grace. Our personal abilities have *nothing* to do with our achievements. His grace unleashes His power in our lives, and it's His power that accomplishes more than we could ever dream of. It can take that mountain we face in life and make it into a mere pebble, or His grace could move it altogether. Either way, it's not about our ability to scale or move mountains, it's His grace that enables His power to flow to us, in us, and through us so that we can conquer the impossible. That's the beauty of grace and another reason why it's such a contributing factor of gentleness.

Grace is the gatekeeper to God's power in our lives, but grace also requires that we recognize our dependency upon God. Again, in 2 Corinthians 12:9, Paul wrote:

> *And He has said to me, "My grace is sufficient for you, for power is perfected in weakness." Most gladly, therefore, I will boast about my weaknesses, so that the power of Christ might dwell in me.*

In other words, Paul was saying that *because* of his weakness, God was able to show His grace and perfect His power in his life. If Paul had accredited his own abilities and showcased his own strengths, he wouldn't have allowed God to work through his life—it would be Paul working through Paul's life, not God.

Not that there's anything wrong with working with our strengths, talents, and abilities, but if we want to see God *really* move through us, we have to get uncomfortable. We have to be willing to go to our weaknesses. Why?

Because then we *have* to depend upon God; we have to step out in faith. When we do this, it's no longer about us and what we're doing; rather, it becomes about God, and if *God* doesn't choose to do something, *everything* will fall apart. That's when His power is undeniable. That's when His power takes over completely, and that's when our human minds meet spiritual dynamite.

That's God's grace.

It's that recognition of our dependence upon God that allows us to see and experience God's grace in our lives. That's why Jesus didn't come for those who believe they've already attained righteousness (see Mark 2:17). It's not that God doesn't *want* to save everyone and work through everyone— including those scribes and Pharisees in Mark 2—it's that they didn't think they needed it. They saw themselves as already perfected and righteous. Therefore, they perceived no need for God's grace, and that mindset blocked God's grace from entering their lives.

It's the recognition that we, alone, are unable, but He is able; that we are insufficient, but He is more than enough that unlocks God's grace to us. After we recognize our dependency upon Him, we must also demonstrate this mindset through our lives. We do this by making the choice to walk in faith, following the leading of His voice one step at a time. It's humility that opens the floodgates of His grace, and it's our faith that activates it. So therefore, if we want to experience and walk in God's grace, we must first be truly humble.

James 4:6 states this principle very clearly: "God is opposed to the proud but gives grace to the humble." This verse is an echo of Psalm 138:6, "He regards the lowly, but the haughty He knows from afar." As we established in Chapter 8, humility carries the connotation of having a low position and is crucial to living a life unified with Christ. A heart of humility, therefore, is the key to unlocking God's grace in our lives.

Without us recognizing our need for Jesus' redemptive power in our lives, we are hopelessly lost, wallowing in the depths of our sin. We need to first acknowledge our need for Him before we can accept His eternal offer of relationship through salvation. It was this exact issue, failure to recognize our need for the Lord, that separated mankind from God all the way back in Genesis.

Adam and Eve believed that they could attain equality with God through a means *outside* of God. It must have been alluring, seductive. To be of equal stature with God? Just by taking one bite of a piece of fruit? We don't need God, just this fruit? The sad truth is, however, they were *already* created in His image and completely unified with God, and they failed to recognize that truth and instead focused upon themselves and their desires. This selfishness then brewed pride in their hearts, and they decided to look to a source outside of God to achieve the fulfillment of what they thought they should be. Instead of placing their faith in God, they placed it in a piece of fruit—an empty promise. That was when the separation between God and humanity occurred: when their hearts decided something along the lines of, *I won't need God, all I'll need is me.*

How often do we fall into this same trap? If we take a hard look at our lives, how often do we honestly fail to rely on God's wisdom and power and instead try to accomplish and achieve in our own strength? It was the pride of man's heart that separated him from God. The outward evidence of that pride was that devastating, spirit-wrenching crunch of forbidden fruit. Pride separated us from God and His grace in the beginning, and it will do so every time we indulge it.

But isn't God omnipotent? Yes, He is. However, out of love for us, His creation, He also gave us free will and will not revoke that gift. He freely offers unity with Him, but if we refuse to cultivate a heart that is conducive to the Lord's presence and power in our lives, He will not supersede our will. Note: I did not say if we try and fail. I said if we *refuse.*

It all boils down to the environment we allow in our hearts: pride or humility? Faith or doubt? Colossians 2:6 says, "Therefore, as you have received Christ Jesus the Lord, so walk in Him." I had read that verse so many times in my life, but the night before I wrote this paragraph, it jumped out at me. *As* I have received Christ, *so* walk in Him. I received Christ through faith and by humbly recognizing how much I need Him. It is the moment we recognize that we are by nature sinners and our only hope is God's power and love, and choose to accept His gift of salvation in faith that we are saved for eternity. It is both—faith and humility—working in tandem in our lives that enable us to experience God's power and love in our lives for the first time, and we are radically changed. Forever.

But He doesn't want to stop there. He wants to continue to pour out His incredible, life-altering, powerful grace in our lives every day. Whether or not that actually happens, though, is up to us. We need to walk in Him through faith and in humility. It is the only way to unlock and activate His grace in our lives and have an intimate relationship with Him. If we only operate in faith and forgo humility, the previously discussed spiritual principle of God's opposition to pride kicks in, and our self-focused choice repels God's grace. As Christians, we do *not* lose salvation, but we do not experience the fullness of God's power in our lives for as long as we refuse to walk in the cover of humility.

Now imagine walking in that power and experiencing that power every day. According to God's will, the sick are healed, prophets speak, and the dead are raised! God's miracles have no end! As incredible as His miracles are for us spiritually and for our physical bodies, His grace can also play another role in our lives, one that I had honestly never considered prior to researching for this chapter.

2 Corinthians 9:8 says, "God is able to make all grace abound to you, so that always having all sufficiency in everything, you may have an abundance for every good deed." I had read that verse so many times in my life and even memorized it along the way for Bible memory in school yet never realized what it so plainly states. God's grace abounds even for our economic and material needs.

The context for this verse is that the Corinthian church was supplying a monetary gift or something similar. Paul was writing to encourage the church in Corinth to have this gift prepared; reminding them in Verse 7 that "God loves a cheerful giver". So, don't begrudge and don't be stingy. It must have been quite a generous gift for Paul to exhort in such a way and to dedicate multiple paragraphs to the topic. In the middle of his exhortation, in Verse 8, he wrote that "it is God's grace that causes this material abundance which is given so the recipient of that grace can bless others." God's favor is the source of His blessings: spiritual, physical, *and* material. Also, note that God blesses us with material blessings, not so we can hoard up wealth for ourselves, but so we can in turn bless others, regardless of whether or not we think they deserve it *and* without expectation of any return. That, after all, is the purpose of grace—to bless and show favor to others.[1,6,7,8] Grace: the unearned, undeserved unlocking of powerful kindness and bountiful blessings to all who come into contact with it. Grace exponentially increases the powerful impact of kindness to those around us which, taken together, are fundamental to the definition of biblical gentleness.

As was previously stated, in order to receive God's grace in your life, we need to humble ourselves. Not think less of ourselves. Not beat ourselves up. That's not humility, that's self-deprecation, and it's destructive. Paul supports this in Colossians 2:23 when he writes:

> *These matters which have, to be sure, the appearance of wisdom in self-made religion and self-abasement and severe treatment of the body but are of no value against fleshly indulgence.*

Therefore, self-deprecation, or thinking less of ourselves and treating ourselves badly, has no actual value. It does not create a clear conduit for God's power, it does not connect us to God, and it does not unleash God's grace in our lives. Instead, to be humble, we need to shift our focus by focusing on ourselves less and Jesus more. Don't focus on what *we* can—or can't—do but instead on what *God* can do. We need to recognize that without Him, those mountains in our lives stay mountains and remain as monuments of the impossible in our lives.

As ancient as the concept of grace is, the empirical research base is surprisingly small. It appears that this particular concept has only gained recent attention and therefore, most of the research available at the time of this writing was focused on establishing methods to uniformly define and measure grace for research purposes.[2,3] That being said, it is *not* surprising that so far empirical research supports a positive role of grace in our lives.

Grace, according to the available research, is multifactorial. Most notably, for me, among the various aspects that the researchers define, there's grace that comes from God, grace we extend to ourselves, and grace that we extend to others.

Researchers from George Fox University conducted studies that showed the religious community, and Christians in particular, had the highest measures of self-reported experience with grace.[4,11] Experiencing grace benefits individuals in that people who report greater experiences with grace tend to have higher self-forgiveness scores, lower rates of depression, and score higher on measures of empathic concern.[11,13,16] Furthermore, those with higher self-reported experiences of grace had higher scores on measures of spiritual well-being and self-reported religiousness.[5,11]

116

Grace benefits interpersonal relationships as well. Dr. Rodger Bufford of George Fox University furthermore showed that after receiving a nine-week grace intervention, a congregation exhibited measurably more grace toward others. This grace directly corresponded to measures of forgiveness toward others.[5] In other words, as their experience with grace increased, so did the amount and depth of forgiveness they were able to extend toward others who had wronged them. Furthermore, while empirical research to directly support this conclusion is not available at this time, in theory, as people reportedly have higher levels of self-forgiveness, less depression, and more empathy, their relationships should begin to flourish and be more satisfying.

This same university, George Fox University, also created a grace intervention which consists of a nine-week sermon series, group Bible studies, and weekly grace practices. I can only assume these are individual and/or group exercises designed to practice concept implementation. Interestingly enough, each article they published showed, undeniably, that at the end of this nine-week intervention, participants had higher self-reported levels of grace. Their experience of grace had increased! Fascinating. By focusing on this attribute over a period of time, their experience and mindset was altered, and in some cases, so was their behavior. Furthermore, they found that married couples had the greatest increase in experiential grace. Unfortunately, they also found that this change waned over time after cessation of the program.[11,13]

What does this mean? I've said it before, and I will say it again here. What we focus our minds on is what we become. We can effect change in our behavior if we intentionally do so, but it must be a regular part of our lives or else the impact is lost. Is it any wonder why God tells us to meditate on Him, His Word, His kindness, and His works? By meditating on His kindness and acts of power, we are in effect, meditating on His grace. It is because of His grace that His kindness flows toward us and His power is unlocked.

God's grace is powerful. It is through His unearned favor that we are saved, that we are able to walk in His power, and experience His love in our lives. Through our humility, His grace is unlocked, unleashed, and causes immense blessings in our physical bodies, our spirits, and even extends to material blessings, according to His will and plans. It is through His grace that we grow in Him and are able to accomplish His plan for our lives. Finally, we are able to grow in our understanding and experience of His grace by

117

consistently meditating on Him and applying His teachings to our lives. Grace, it's for more than just salvation; it's God's blessings and power released in your life.

Grace is a potent facet of living a life of gentleness. The concept of grace takes gentleness's acts of kindness and release of blessings and mixes in the notion that these benefits are unearned. Imagine the impact of a deluge of kindness and blessing on a recipient that knows he/she is completely undeserving. Wow! Grace takes the impact of the attribute of gentleness and revs up the power.

Challenge Questions:

1. In what areas in my life have I been relying on myself instead of God?

2. In what areas of my life have I been relying on outside sources instead of God? Think jobs, money, and other people.

3. In what areas have I allowed fear, doubt, or self-focus to drive my decisions instead of reliance upon God and His Word?

4. What areas in my life can I increase my dependence upon God? Be specific.

5. What steps can I take toward increasing my reliance upon God in the areas I just listed? Be specific.

6. Find at least one Bible verse about God's grace. Copy it and meditate upon it.

7. What areas and times in my life have I experienced God's grace? Be specific.

8. I can show my family more grace by _____.

9. I can show my coworkers more grace by _____.

10. I can show my friends more grace by _____.

11. I can show other people I come into contact with more grace by _____.

Social Connection

From the get-go, humanity was created for social bonding. After creating the universe and all the plants and animals on Earth, God made a man for the sole purpose of having a relationship with him. But man's need for connection went beyond that. Even with a perfect relationship with God, God *still* said that it wasn't good for man to be alone, and the first woman entered the scene. Therefore, while we are completely dependent on God and absolutely need to have a relationship with Him, we also have relationships with other people. And how can we truly express gentleness, or any other spiritual fruit for that matter, without social connection? After all, fruit is meant to be taken off whatever tree (or person!) grows it, and given to others for their enjoyment and edification.

Perhaps one of the clearest examples of our need for and the benefits of connection comes from the tiniest of us all—premature infants. Years ago, NICU babies were sequestered away in their germ-free cradles. Thought too fragile to tolerate human contact, these precious little ones fought solo, aided only by medical technology and pharmaceuticals. Physical touch was prohibited, since we knew that as human beings, we carry viruses and bacteria which are harmful to these babies with underdeveloped immune systems. All of that changed in 1995.

Twin girls were born twelve weeks prematurely, and one was not expected to make it. The nurses fought for permission to put them into the same incubator and, thankfully, won. Staff were amazed as they watched the larger, stronger twin put her arm over her sister. After receiving this simple touch, the struggling twin's heart rate and body temperature stabilized.[2] Hospital policies were changed immediately, and research was done on what is now known as *kangaroo contact.*

The research on kangaroo contact, or skin-to-skin contact from caregiver to infant, alone attests to the impact of connection through physical touch. Studies done on kangaroo contact during infancy show that this simple gesture has the ability to promote bonding and attunement from mother to child. And, amazingly, the benefits go beyond mother-to-child bonding; they extend to the baby as well. Provision of kangaroo contact during infancy has been shown to promote better sleep patterns, problem solving skills, and better responses to stress in babies.[3] But are the benefits of touch limited to infants and their mothers? Absolutely not.

Touch is associated with reducing negative stimuli, such as stress, in adults too.[9] One study, led by Dr. James Coan from the University of Virginia, even found that it can reduce our perception of physical pain! This study used married couples and showed that the impact of this benefit is strongest when the relationship is intimate and when both people are highly satisfied with the relationship.[1] Guess there's a reason why we reach out with our hands and arms when someone is physically injured; physical contact for the purpose of comfort when experiencing pain or stress isn't just for little ones.

But just how does this happen? What processes occur within our bodies when we touch one another that are capable of producing these results? For one, the reward center of our brain activates, which means we feel good and happy when we touch someone.[11] And two…remember oxytocin…warm fuzzies? Whether or not we actually experience the warm fuzzy sensation, oxytocin is released when we physically touch someone. As already discussed earlier in this book, in addition to reducing stress, the release of oxytocin promotes bonding and reduces blood pressure and inflammation, all of which contribute to reduction of the perception of pain and stress.[5,7,10]

Touch is powerful, no doubt about it, but it isn't the *only* way we connect as human beings. We also connect through communication, both verbal and nonverbal. One way we connect nonverbally is through empathy which enables us to share ourselves on an emotional level. It goes beyond understanding the words coming out of someone's mouth all the way to actually experiencing the feelings that someone else is experiencing. It's an illogical connection on the level of the subconscious. And it's powerful.

Empathy can make us smile when we feel down, and it can move us to take action to alleviate someone else's suffering or burden…but it can also take a little tiff and blow it up into the fight of the century. Its impact may be subtle. The effects may be fleeting. But our ability to process someone else's emotions as if they were our own, *all the way down to our brainwaves,* is one way to build strong connections.[6] It would be challenging to deepen our relationships with others if we were unable to relate on a visceral level. I imagine it would be similar to having a relationship with a robot. Sure, there's communication, but clearly no connection, and without a connection, there is no growth, interpersonal *or* intrapersonal.

Connecting with other people enables growth; not just an ever-deepening level of interpersonal emotional and mental intimacy, but also growth for each person individually. When someone invests in another person, they are demonstrating that they believe in him/her. Without a doubt, that confidence provides support and can offer the mental and emotional boost needed to take steps that would otherwise go untrodden. This confidence boost then provides the impetus that propels someone forward which in turn facilitates growth within that person.

I was on my honeymoon in Maui, and my husband and I decided to take an adventurous guided spelunking tour of an underground lava tube. Seeing a volcano's guts was incredible and a memory I will never forget in large part because of one tiny, but decisive, moment. We were wriggling our way upwards through the tube and came to a point where there was a large gap between where we were and where we needed to go. It was dim, but even so, I could tell that the bottom was a place I didn't want to go—there would be no return. I didn't scare easily when it came to adventures of this nature, but I was terrified now. I thought of the future dreams my new husband and I had and wondered if they were going to be lost in this dark chasm. Nevertheless, I decided to go for it. Why? Because my husband was there. I remember feeling secure with his presence and feeling like even though this venture was a bit too frightening for me, I could do anything if he was there with me. And if I faltered? I believed in my heart of hearts he would be there to save me. That's the power of social support.

Social support has been shown to reduce distress, stress, increase longevity, and promote good health.[8] How do we provide this type of support for one another? The first thing most of us think of when it comes to supporting one another probably has to do with the dark times: death, job loss, or a serious illness. But it doesn't have to be limited to the valleys; we

121

can support each other in our pinnacle moments as well. For example, when a friend or spouse gets a promotion or an award, wholeheartedly and genuinely rejoice with him/her. We can also encourage and affirm his or her goals and dreams, regardless of whether or not they wind up working out.[8]

Providing support to each other through both positive and negative circumstances deepens our levels of intimacy and can help us achieve what we never thought possible. I doubt I would have had the courage to attempt to cross that chasm on my honeymoon without the support of my husband. The continual, daily support between my husband and me has been invaluable throughout our marriage, as we have crossed over more than one treacherous path, almost all of which were unseen to the physical eye. Each one of the obstacles we have encountered has enriched and deepened our relationship with its unique imprint in our shared memories.

While a Christ-centered marriage is one source of positive social support, friends are another invaluable source. I cannot tell you how many times I have been ministered to, encouraged, and lovingly nudged toward my goals by my inner circle of friends, and I'm not the only one who benefitted from friendship. While history is full of examples of friends bolstering friends, within the pages of the Bible we find one beautiful, quintessential example of the power of friendship in the story of David and Jonathan.

These two men couldn't have come from more disparate backgrounds. Jonathan was the son of the king, living in luxury, his every want and need met. Then we have David, a poor shepherd boy, often found by himself in the fields, where he fended for himself and his sheep. Yet these two find their paths colliding in 1 Samuel 18, and in the first verse, it says, "The soul of Jonathan was knit to the soul of David, and Jonathan loved him as himself." Despite the differences in their backgrounds and social statuses, these two men just clicked. The next chapters of 1 Samuel highlight how these two men developed such a deep bond that they entered into a covenant of friendship together in 1 Samuel 20. A prince and a poor shepherd boy found themselves supporting one another through battles, through love and marriage, and even providing life-sparing safety through King Saul's betrayal of David (see 1 Samuel 20). I imagine Jonathan's steadfast brotherly love toward David through his trials was a great source of strength and helped him dig deep into the grit of his soul to push forward so he could ultimately become the King of Israel that God planned for him to be.

Navigating life together with another person who provides true social support can empower us to successfully traverse those challenges that ultimately shape and refine us into the best we can be so we can accomplish what God has in store for us. After all, according to Proverbs 27:17, "Iron sharpens iron, so one man sharpens another." Thankfully, social support also helps make the process of conquering life's challenges more enjoyable and can even give us more time to enjoy the fruit grown from them.[8]

But how do we get there? How do we take a complete stranger and forge a connection deep enough so that this level of sharing and support is possible? By mixing the ingredients of time and trust. My experience says that there really aren't any shortcuts. While it is possible to have one of those instant magical connections with someone, true depth in a relationship takes time. Shortcuts can lead to painful pitfalls.

Building trust can be scary. I remember as a child, one of my first experiences with an adrenaline rush was through "trust falls." It was a delicious blend of anticipation and fear which I repeated over and over and over again with anyone who would indulge me. I kept raising the stakes higher, finding steps and then structures to fall from into the arms of my trusted friends or family. But here's the thing about trust—someone has to take the plunge. This can be overwhelming and terrifying, especially if we've been hurt in the past, but we need to remember that the rewards of a mutually beneficial, intimate relationship are exponential and reaped over a lifetime.

There's no need to start with jumping over a chasm inside a volcano. If trust is difficult, start slowly. Just as I gradually heightened the stakes for my trust falls, it's often best to gradually heighten the emotional intimacy stakes, bit by bit, in select relationships. Perhaps one day, that jump over the pit of blackness in a test of ultimate trust won't be quite as intimidating. Just don't forget, there's no need to rush the process, because building trust also requires the second ingredient in forging deep social connections…time.

Time is essential to relationships. It's hard with busy schedules and so many things pulling us in different directions, but there's no substitute for time when building a relationship. We need to make the time to be together and to talk. I'm going to go say something that may be shocking, so sit down if you aren't already. Social media is NOT a replacement for face-to-face contact.

Social media is a great way to check in with people, get to know them initially, and to acquire material for conversations (i.e., vacation or project photos make nice conversation pieces), but it *should not* replace a more direct means of communication. Even email and texting, while more direct, cannot replace spoken communication. There are nuances present within the tones of our voices that shade meaning and, I feel, can bring us closer together by allowing us to glimpse each other's personalities and the realm of the unspoken. We simply can't do this with black and white letters. To make a connection stronger, and even more personal, we also really need to make time for face-to-face contact, if possible. Again, our facial expressions and body language lend itself to coloring our conversations and adding a depth not present with vocal communication only. Face-to-face contact also enables us to experience a more substantial subconscious connection through empathy with the other person. Finally, when we are physically present with someone, we open up the possibility of touch (when done appropriately and respectfully within biblically-defined boundaries of our relationship). And we've already talked about the power of touch.

Considering the fact that it requires time, and lots of it, to establish deep social connections, it bears the question: what about relationship longevity? Don't we eventually get tired of our relationships? As people we tire easily of our new electronics, cars, and houses, especially when the newest, hottest version becomes available. Do we get tired of other people, thereby causing our interest and connection to wane?

This phenomenon, well-known to all of us, is called *hedonic adaptation*. Hedonic adaptation prevents us from continuing to derive pleasure from objects over time. We adjust to having that new car, outfit, pair of shoes, or gadget, and come to assimilate that item into our daily lives. When it's no longer new, we stop savoring its presence in our lives; instead, we simply pass it by and take that once-coveted object for granted. Fortunately, the research shows that this phenomenon does not happen in our relationships provided we are not self-centered and our relationships are not simply self-serving. This means that authentic relationships are set apart from every single other facet of our lives.[8] Relationships are, in short, special and should be treated that way. So, the next time we decide to get ourselves that fancy whatchamacallit, we should invite a friend to come along and invest in what really matters.

The concept of social connection was saved for last in this book because, as I pondered the various aspects of gentleness, they all seemed to lead to the one thing God made us for: relationships. The most important relationship humanity will ever have is the one we share with God. God's extension of grace toward us is an incredible demonstration of His power and love, and it sets into motion the mind-blowing reality that we can—and do—have a very real connection with Him. As we grow in intimacy in our relationship with the Lord, He is able to transform us into someone we never would have imagined ourselves to be.

This is the reality His gentleness engenders in our lives. His power, grace, kindness, leadership, humility, and love blend together to nurture the trust required for us to take that leap to connect with Him and make ourselves completely vulnerable and dependent upon Him. The transformation we experience in our lives is entirely dependent upon the depth of our reliance upon Him and our continual fellowship with His Spirit. Psalm 37:5-6a says, "Commit your way to the Lord, trust also in Him, and He will do it. He will bring forth your righteousness as the light...." Our metamorphosis from carnality to maturity in Christ is contingent upon our connection to Him and its depth. This passage says that we need to *commit* our lives and plans to the Lord. Not halfway and not haphazardly—we need to go all in, and when we do, we demonstrate our trust in the Lord through our everyday lives. Furthermore, in this passage, God also gives us a promise when we walk in this type of faith—He will produce righteousness in our lives, a righteousness that radiates God's light to those around us. As Jesus says in John 15:5, He is the vine, and we are the branches. Just as a branch cannot possibly grow and morph into a mature appendage with leaves and fruit without being fully connected and engaged with the vine, we cannot develop and transform without complete trust and dependency upon *and* intimate connection with Him.

While our relationship with God should always remain our number one priority, He placed us here on Earth with other people for the purpose of relationship. Otherwise, why would He have bothered to create Eve? God wants us to connect with other people to share our hearts, our visions, and our lives. He wants us to support each other, celebrate together, contrast and complement one another, and grow together.

The attributes wrapped up in gentleness are crucial for us to initiate, maintain, and deepen our connections with each other. The absence of self-control, kindness, humility, and grace in anyone's life would certainly end in complete isolation in one form or another. However, if we choose to live a life of gentleness—a life of self-control, humility, grace, and kindness while wielding leadership and power—it's like adding fertilizer to the garden of social bonding. Being able to connect in such a way that allows someone to speak into another person's life, lift them up, and guide them in a positive direction has untold value for both the giver and receiver of biblical gentleness. Surely, they will reap abundant blessings in their lives.

Discipleship and friendship can establish incredible levels of intimacy and help both involved develop beyond what they would be able to do alone. It is through this development that we are able to have a greater demonstration of God's love and power in and through our lives, thereby having a greater impact on those around us. In the beginning, God's design for humanity started with relationships, and in the end, God's plans are achieved through relationships.

Challenge Questions:

1. When did I experience God's gentleness in my life? How did this experience impact me immediately? What impact did it have on me over time?
2. What are my closest relationships? What enabled me to build a strong connection with these people? What can I do to continue to deepen those connections?
3. What qualities do I look for when establishing a friendship or relationship? Does my own life exhibit these qualities? What can I do to begin to grow or further develop these attributes in myself?
4. Do I find it easy or hard to trust others? If I find it hard, what can I do to help build trust with one person in my life? If I find it easy, what can I do to verify that another person is trustworthy?
5. Have I had a relationship that promoted positive, personal growth? What was it about that relationship that enabled this growth to occur?

6. What longstanding relationships do I have (preferably greater than ten years)? What contributed to its longevity? To its success? How has this relationship impacted my life?

7. Is there someone in my life right now that is going through a difficult time? How can I show reliable and gentle support to that person?

8. Is there someone in my life right now that is experiencing success? How can I show reliable and gentle support to that person?

9. What method of communication do I typically use to connect with people (think about social media, texting, voice calls, face-to-face)? How can I use social media and text communication methods to deepen my relationships outside of those means? How can I integrate more face-to-face time with others?

10. About how much time do I spend on the different things I do in my life? Log your actual times for a week or two. Compare the estimates with the log. Where does most of my time go? What does this reveal about my priorities? What we spend our time (and discretionary money) on often reveals our true priorities. Keep this in mind for the following question.

11. What are my true priorities? Look back over your log from #10. Does my use of time reflect what I feel to be my true priorities? If not, what can I do to make my true priorities my real priorities?

12. What makes me feel valued? What makes the people closest to me feel valued? How can I show these individuals that I truly value them? Make a list and include steps, if necessary.

Epilogue

When God created us, He meant for us to have intimate and healthy relationships with Himself and with our fellow human beings. It is only through these relationships that we grow and flourish. Experiencing God's gentleness in our lives provides a perfect example for us and helps us to cultivate gentleness in our lives. As we produce gentleness in our lives, we are able to cultivate our relationships, and this enables us to accomplish God's ultimate purpose—a relationship with Him and relationships with others. Gentleness. It's not pallid—it's power's best kept secret.

ABOUT
KHARIS PUBLISHING

KHARIS PUBLISHING is an independent, traditional publishing house with a core mission to publish impactful books, and channel proceeds into establishing mini-libraries or resource centers for orphanages in developing countries, so these kids will learn to read, dream, and grow. Every time you purchase a book from Kharis Publishing or partner as an author, you are helping give these kids an amazing opportunity to read, dream, and grow. Kharis Publishing is an imprint of Kharis Media LLC. Learn more at https://www.kharispublishing.com.

Works Cited

It's All Greek

1. Acton, J. "Lord Acton Quote Archive." *Acton Institute,*
    2018. Retrieved from https://acton.org/research/lord-acton-quote
    archive. Accessed 23 April 2018.

2. "Epieikés." HELPS Word-studies. 2011. Retrieved from *BibleHub,*
    http://biblehub.com/greek/1933.htm

3. "Épios." HELPS Word-studies. 2011. Retrieved from
    BibleHub, http://biblehub.com/greek/2261.htm

4. Philippians 4:3 Commentaries. *BibleHub,*
    http://biblehub.com/commentaries/philippians/4-
    3.htm

5. "Praüs." HELPS Word-studies. 2011. Retrieved from
    BibleHub, http://biblehub.com/greek/4239.htm

6. "Suzugos." HELPS Word-studies. 2011. Retrieved from *BibleHub,*
    http://biblehub.com/str/greek/4805.htm

7. Vail, Lesley. Personal Communication.

8. Vine, W.E., et al. "Gentle." *Vine's Complete Expository
    Dictionary of Old and New Testament Words.*
    Thomas Nelson, Inc., 1996.

9. Vine, W.E., et al. "Meek." *Vine's Complete Expository
    Dictionary of Old and New Testament Words.*
    Thomas Nelson, Inc., 1996.

Exploring Hebrew

1. "About the Hebrew Language." *Mechanical Translation of Genesis*. n.d. http://www.ancient-hebrew.org/mt/index.html

2. Ahani, A., et al. "Quantitative Change of EEG and Respiration Signals During Mindfulness and Meditation." *Journal of Neuroengineering and Rehabilitation*. 11:87, 2014.

3. "Alluwph." *Strong's Exhaustive Concordance Updated Edition*. Retrieved from *BibleHub*. *http://biblehub.com/strongs/hebrew/441.htm*

4. Barnes, V., et al. "Impact of Transcendental Meditation on Cardiovascular Function at Rest and During Acute Stress in Adolescents with High Normal Blood Pressure." *Journal of Psychosomatic Research*. vol. 51, no. 4, 2001, pp. 597-605. MS

5. Barnes, V., et al. "Impact of Breathing Awareness Meditation on Ambulatory Blood Pressure and Sodium Handling in Prehypertensive African-American Adolescents." *Ethnicity and Disease*. vol. 18, no. 1, 2008, pp. 1-5. MS

6. Bernardi, L., et al. "Effect of Rosary Prayer and Yoga Mantras on Autonomic Cardiovascular Rhythms: Comparative Study." *BMJ*. 323, 2001, pp. 1446-1449.

7. Black, D. and Slavich, G. "Mindfulness Meditation and the Immune System: A Systematic Review of Randomized Controlled Trials." *Annals of the New York Academy of Science*. vol. 1371, no. 1, 2016, pp. 13-24. doi: 10.1111/nyas.12998. MS

8. Braeken, Marijke, et al. "Potential Benefits of Mindfulness During Pregnancy on Maternal Autonomic Nervous System Function and Infant Development." *Psychophysiology*. vol. 54, 2016, pp. 279-288. doi: 10.1111/psyp.12782

9. Chaddha, A. "Slow Breathing and Cardiovascular Disease." *International Journal of Yoga*. vol. 8, no. 2, 2015, pp. 142-143. doi: 10/4103/09736131.158484

10. Creswell, J.D., et al. "Brief Mindfulness Meditation Training Alters Psychological and Neuroendocrine Responses to Evaluative Stress." *Psychoneuroendocrinology*. vol. 44, 2014, pp. 1-12. doi:10.1016/j.psyneuen.2014.02.007

11. Ditto, B., et al. "Short-Term Autonomic and Cardiovascular Effects of Mindfulness Body Scan Meditation." *Annals of Behavioral Medicine.* vol. 32, no. 3, 2006, pp. 227-234.

12. "Epieikés." *Strong's Exhaustive Concordance Updated Edition.* Retrieved from *BibleHub.* http://biblehub.com/str/greek/1933.htm

13. Frederickson, B., et al. "Open Hearts Build Lives: Positive Emotions, Induced Through Loving Kindness Meditation, Build Consequential Personal Resources." *Journal of Personality and Social Psychology.* vol. 95, no. 5, 2008, pp. 1045-1062. doi: 10.1037/a0013262

14. "Gentle." *NAS Exhaustive Concordance.* Zondervan, 1998.

15. Newberg, A., et al. "Cerebral Blood Flow Differences Between Long-Term Meditators and Non Meditators." *Consciousness and Cognition.* 2010. doi: 10.1016/j.concog.2010.05.003

16. Nyklíček, I., et al. "Mindfulness-Based Stress Reduction and Physiological Activity

    During Acute Stress: A Randomized Controlled Trial." *Health Psychology.* Advance online publication 2013. doi:10.1037/a0032200

17. Pace, T., et al. "Effect of Compassion Meditation on Neuroendocrine, Innate Immune and Behavioral Responses to Psychosocial Stress." *Psychoneuroendocrinology.* vol. 34, no. 1, 2009, pp. 87-98. doi: 10.1016/j.psycneuen.2008.08/011

18. Peng, C., et al. "Heart Rate Dynamics During Three Forms of Meditation." *International Journal of Cardiology.* vol. 95, 2004, pp. 19-27. doi: 10.1016/j.ijcard.2003.02.006

19. "Rabah." *Strong's Exhaustive Concordance Updated Edition.* Retrieved from *BibleHub.* https://biblehub.com/hebrew/7235.htm

20. Tan, L., et al. "Brief Mindfulness Meditation Improves Mental State Attribution and Empathizing." *PLoS*

ONE. vol. 9, no. 10, 2014, pp. 1-5. doi:
10.1372/journalpone.0110510

21. Tang, Y., et al. "Short-Term Meditation Training
Improves Attention and Self-Regulation." *PNAS.*
vol. 104, no. 43, 2007, pp. 17152-17156. doi:
10.1073/pnas.0707678104

22. Taren, A., et al. "Mindfulness Meditation Training
Alters Stress-Related Amygdala Resting State
Functional Connectivity: A Randomized
Controlled Trial." *Social Cognitive and Affective
Neuroscience.* 2015, pp. 1758-1768. doi:
10.1093/scan/nsv066

23. Taylor, V., et al. "Impact of Meditation Training on the
Default Mode Network During a Restful State."
SCAN. vol. 8, 2013, pp. 4-14. doi:
10/1093/scan/nsr087

24. *The Holy Bible, King James Version.* Cambridge
Edition: 1769; *King James Bible Online,* 2020.
www.kingjamesbibleonline.org.

25. Wells, R., et al. "Meditation's Impact on Default Mode
Network and Hippocampus in Mild Cognitive
Impairment: A Pilot Study." *Neuroscience.* vol.
556, 2013, pp. 15-19. doi: 10/1016/j.neulet.10/001

26. Wu, S. and Lo, P. "Inward Attention Meditation
Increases Parasympathetic Activity: Study Based
on Heart Rate Variability." *Biomedical Research.*
vol. 29, no. 5, 2008, pp. 245-250.

27. Yang, C., et al. "State and Training Effects of
Mindfulness Meditation on Brain Networks
Reflect Neuronal Mechanisms of Its
Antidepressant Effect." *Neural Plasticity.* 2016,
pp. 1-14. doi: 10/1155/2016/9504642

Down to the Letter

1. "About the Hebrew Language." *Mechanical Translation of Genesis.* n.d.
http://www.ancient-hebrew.org/mt/index.html

2. Barsade, S. "The Ripple Effect: Emotional Contagion and Its Influence on Group Behavior." *Administrative Science Quarterly*. vol. 47, no. 4, 2002, pp. 644-675.

3. Baskin, J. and Seeskin, K. *The Cambridge Guide to Jewish History, Religion, and Culture*. Cambridge University Press, 2010. pp. 313, 344.

4. Bushman, B., et al. "Do People Aggress to Improve Their Mood? Catharsis Beliefs, Affect Regulation Opportunity, and Aggressive Responding." *Journal of Personality and Social Psychology*. vol. 82, no. 1, 2001, pp. 17-32.

5. Carlsmith, K., et al. "The Paradoxical Consequences of Revenge." *Journal of Personality and Social Psychology*. vol. 95, no. 6, 2008, pp. 1316-1324.

6. Chester, D. and DeWall, C.N. "The Pleasure of Revenge: Retaliatory Aggression Arises from a Neural Imbalance Toward Reward." *Social Cognitive and Affective Neuroscience*. 2016, pp.1173-1182. doi: 10.1093/scan/nsv082

7. Crystal, D. *Spell it Out: The Curious Enthralling, and Extraordinary Story of English Spelling*. St. Martin's Press, 2012. pp. 26-31

8. Hasan, Y., et al. "Violent Video Games Stress People Out and Make Them More Aggressive." Author's manuscript.

9. "Jewish Practices and Rituals: Covering of the Head." *Jewish Virtual Library*, n.d. http://www.jewishvirtuallibrary.org/covering-of the-head

10. Knight, D. and Levine, A. *The Meaning of the Bible: What the Jewish Scriptures and Christian Old Testament can Teach Us*. HarperCollins, 2011. pp. 102-3

11. Korb, S., et al. "Reappraising the Voices of Wrath." *Social Cognitive and Affective Neuroscience*. 2015, pp. 1644-1660. doi: 10.1093/scan/nsv051

12. "Maaneh." *Biblehub.com*, n.d. http://biblehub.com/hebrew/4617.htm

13. Ouaknin, M. *Mysteries of the Alphabet*. Abbeville Press, 1999. pp. 118-123, 172-173, 191, 222, 229, 264

14. Pratico, G. and Van Pelt, M. *Basics of Biblical Hebrew, 2nd edition.* Zondervan, 2007. pp. 9, 63-4.

15. Rosen, M. *Alphabetical: How Every Letter Tells a Story.* Counterpoint Press, 2015. pp.64, 94, 130, 160, 176, 204, 218, 268

16. Sacks, D. *Language Visible.* Broadway Books, 2013. pp. 52-53, 114, 204, 217-18, 233, 241, 251, 261, 273, 283, 293, 305, 313

17. "Writing." *Encyclopaedia Judaica,* 2008. Retrieved from *Jewish Virtual Library.* http://www.jewishvirtuallibrary.org/writing. Accessed 3 February 2018.

Power

1. Acton, J. "Lord Acton Quote Archive." *Acton Institute,* 2018. Retrieved from https://acton.org/research/lord-acton-quote archive. Accessed 23 April 2018.

2. Anderson, C. and Berdahl, J. "The Experience of Power: Examining the Effects of Power on Approach and Inhibition Tendences." *Journal of Personality and Social Psychology,* 2002, vol. 83, no. 6, pp. 1362-1377, doi: 10.1037//00223514.83.6.1362

3. Aguinis, H., et al. "Effects of Nonverbal Behavior on Perception of Power Bases." *The Journal of Social Psychology,* 1998, vol. 138, no. 4, pp. 455-469

4. Berry, D. and McArthur, L. "Perceiving Character in Faces: The Impact of Age-Related Craniofacial Changes on Social Perception." *Psychological Bulletin,* 1986, vol. 100, no. 1, pp. 3-18.

5. de Zavala, A. et al. "Yoga Poses Increase Subjective Energy and State Self-Esteem in Comparison to 'Power Poses.'" *Frontiers in Psychology,* 2017, vol. 8:752, doi:10.3389/fpsyg.2017.00752

6. Carney, D., et al. "Beliefs About the Nonverbal Expression of Power." *Journal of Nonverbal Behavior,* 2005, vol. 29, no. 2, pp. 105-124, doi:10.1007/s10919-005-2743-z

7. Cialdini, R. *Influence: The Psychology of Persuasion, Revised,* 2007. pp. 226-227.

8. Cialdini, R. *Pre-suasion: A Revolutionary Way to Influence and Persuade,* Simon and Schuster, 2016. pp. 54-56.

9. Cuddy, A. *Presence: Bringing Your Boldest Self to Your Biggest Challenges,* Little, Brown and Co., 2015.

10. Cuddy, A., et al. "Preparatory Power Posing Affects Nonverbal Presence and Job Interview Performance." *Journal of Applied Psychology,* 2015, vol. 100, no. 4. pp. 1286-1295. doi: 10.1037/a0038543

11. Cuddy, A., et al. "Power Posing: Brief Nonverbal Displays Affect Neuroendocrine Levels and Risk Tolerance." *Psychological Science,* 2010, vol. 21, no.10, pp.1363-1368. doi: 10.1177/0956797610383437

12. DeGroot, T. and Motowildo, S. "Why Visual and Verbal Interview Cues Can Affect Interviewers' Judgments and Predict Job Performance." *Journal of Applied Psychology,* 1999, vol. 84, no. 6, pp. 986-993.

13. Galinsky, A., et al. "Power Reduces the Press of the Situation: Implications for Creativity Conformity, and Dissonance." *Journal of Personality and Social Psychology,* 2008, vol. 95, no. 6, pp. 1450 1466. doi:10.1037/a0012633

14. Goleman, D. *Working with Emotional Intelligence,* Bantam Books, 1998. pp. 68, 71.

15. Hall, J., et al. "Nonverbal Behavior and the Vertical Dimension of Social Relations: A Meta-Analysis." *Psychological Bulletin,* 2005, vol. 131, no. 6, pp. 898-924. doi: 10.1037/0033 2909.131.6.898

16. "Heart." *Baker's Evangelical Dictionary of Biblical Theology,* Baker Books, 1996. Retrieved from https://www.biblestudytools.com/dictionary/heart/

17. Hedges, K. *The Power of Presence: Unlock Your Potential to Influence and Engage Others,* American Management Association, 2012. pp. 11-15, 45-46.

18. Huang,L. "Powerful Postures vs. Powerful Roles." *Psychological Science,* 2011, vol. 22, no. 1, pp. 85-102. doi:10.1177/0956797610391912

19. Gendolla, G. "On the Impact of Mood on Behavior: An Integrative Theory and Review." *Review of General Psychology,* vol. 4, no. 4, pp. 378=408. doi:10.1037//1089-2680.4.4.378

20. Kacewicz, E., et al. "Pronoun Use Reflects Social Standings in Hierarchies." *Journal of Language and Social Psychology.* 2013, pp. 1-19. doi: 10.1177/0261927X13502654

21. Kang, S. "Power Affects Performance When the Pressure is On: Evidence for Low-Power Threat and High-Power Lift." *Personality and Social Psychology,* 2015, vol. 41, no. 5, pp. 726-735. doi:10.1177/0146167215577365

22. Karremans, J. and Smith, P. "Having the Power to Forgive: When the Experience of Power Increases Interpersonal Forgiveness." *Personality and Social Psychology,* 2010, vol. 36, no. 8, pp. 1010-1023. doi:10.1177/0146167210376761

23. "Lebab." *Strong's Exhaustive Concordance, Updated Edition.* Retrieved from *BibleHub*

    https://biblehub.com/hebrew/3824.htm

24. Mast, M., et al. "Give a Person Power and He or She Will Show Interpersonal Sensitivity: The Phenomenon and Its Why and When." *Journal of Personality and Social Psychology,* 2009, vol. 97, no. 5, pp. 835-850. doi:10.1037/a0016234

25. Peschard, V., et al. "Involuntary Processing of Social Dominance Cues from Bimodal Face-Voice Displays. *Cognition and Emotion,* 2016. doi: 10.1080/02699931.2016.1266304

26. "Power." *Merriam-Webster.* 2018, https://www.merriamwebster.com/ dictionary/power. Accessed 7 April 2018.

27. Puts, D., et al. "Dominance and the Evolution of Sexual Dimorphism in Human Voice Pitch." *Evolution*

and Human Behavior, 2006, 27, pp. 283-296 doi:
10.1016/j.evolhumbehav.2005.11.003

28. Re, D. and Rule, N. "Predicting Firm Success From the
Facial Appearance of Chief Executive Officers
of Non-Profit Organizations." *Perception,* 2016,
vol. 45, no.10, pp. 1137-1150. doi:
10.1177/0301006616652043

29. Smith, P., et al. "Lacking Power Impairs Executive
Function." *Psychological Science,* 2008, vol. 19,
no. 5, pp. 441-449.

30. Smith, P., et al. "Powerful People Make Good
Decisions Even When They Consciously Think."
Psychological Science, 2008, vol. 19, no. 12, pp.
1258-1259.

31. Stel, M., et al. "Lowering the Pitch of Your Voice
Makes You Feel More Powerful and Think More
Abstractly." *Social Psychological and
Personality Science,* 2012, vol. 3, no. 4, pp. 497
502. doi: 10.1177/1948550611427610

32. Vacharkulksemsuk, T., et al. "Dominant, Open
Nonverbal Displays are Attractive at Zero
Acquaintance." *PNAS,* 2016, vol. 113, no. 15, pp.
4009-4014. doi:10.1073/pnas.1508932113/
/DCSupplemental

33. Vaish, A., et al. "Not All Emotions Are Created Equal:
The Negativity Bias in Social-Emotional
Development." *Psychological Bulletin,* 2008, vol.
134, no. 3, pp. 383-403. doi:10.1037/0033
2909.134.3.383

34. Wong, E., et al. "A Face Only an Investor Could Love:
CEO's Facial Structure Predicts Their Firms'
Financial Performance." *Psychological Science,*
2011, vol. 22, no.12, pp. 1478-1483. doi:
10.1177/0956797611418838

35. Zuckerman, M., et al. "Effects of Attractiveness and
Maturity of Face and Voice on Interpersonal
Impressions." *Journal of Research in
Personality,* 1995, vol. 29, no. 2, pp. 253-272.

An Overview of Leadership. Positive Leadership Styles. Godly Leadership. Making the Connections.

1. Berry, D. "Accuracy in Social Perception: Contributions of Facial and Vocal Information." *Journal of Personality and Social Psychology*, 1991, vol. 61, no. 2 pp. 298-307.

2. Berry, D. and McArthur, L. "Perceiving Character in Faces: The Impact of Age-Related Craniofacial Changes on Social Perception." *Psychological Bulletin*, 1986, vol. 100, no. 1, pp. 3-18.

3. Calbi, M., et al. "'Embodied Body Language': An Electrical Neuroimaging Study with Emotional Faces and Bodies." *Scientific Reports*, 2017, vol. 7:6875 doi: 10/1038/s41598-017-07262-0

4. Cerit, Y. "The Effects of Servant Leadership Behaviours of School Principals on Teachers' Job Satisfaction." *Educational Management Administration and Leadership*, 2009, vol. 37, no. 5, pp. 600-623. doi: 10.1177/1741143209339650

5. Cialdini, R. *Pre-suasion: A Revolutionary Way to Influence and Persuade*, Simon and Schuster, 2016. pp. 214-223.

6. Cuddy, A., et al. "Connect, Then Lead." *Harvard Business Review*, 2013, pp. 55-61.

7. Cuddy, A. *Presence: Bringing Your Boldest Self to Your Biggest Challenges*, Little, Brown and Co., 2015.

8. Diano, M, et al. "Dynamic Changes in Amygdala Psychophysiological Connectivity Reveal Distinct Neural Networks for Facial Expressions of Basic Emotions." *Scientific Reports*, 2017, vol.7:45260. doi: 10/1038,srep45260

9. Ekman, P. *Emotions Revealed*, Henry Holt and Company, LLC, 2004.

10. "Empathy." *Oxford Living Dictionaries*. Oxford University Press, 2018. Retrieved from https://en.oxforddictionaries.com/definition/empathy. Accessed 11 April 2018.

11. Gaal, Rachel. "The Collapse of the Tacoma Narrows Bridge." *APS News*. 2016, vol. 25, no. 10. Retrieved from https://www.aps.org/publications

/apsnews201611/physicshistory.cfm/. Accessed
7 April 2018.

12. Gillath, O., et al. "Attachment, Authenticity, and
    Honesty: Dispositional and Experimentally
    Induced Security Can Reduce Self- and Other
    Deception." *Journal of Personality and Social
    Psychology*, 2010, vol. 98, no. 5, pp. 841-855.
    doi: 10.1037/a0019206

13. Goldman, A. and de Vignemont, F. "Is Social
    Cognition Embodied?" *Trends in Cognitive
    Science*, 2009, vol. 13, no. 4, pp.154-159.

14. Goleman, D. *Social Intelligence: The New Science of
    Human Relationships*, Bantam Dell, 2006.

15. Goleman, D., et al. *Primal Leadership: Learning to
    Lead with Emotional Intelligence*, Harvard
    Business School Press, 2002.

16. Goleman, D. *Working with Emotional Intelligence*,
    Bantam Books, 1998. pp. 51-53, 140-142,167-168.

17. Harrison, N., et al. "The Embodiment of Emotional
    Feelings in the Brain." *Journal of Neuroscience*,
    2010, vol. 30, no. 38, pp. 12878-12884. doi:
    10/1523/JNEUROSCI.1725-10/2010

18. Hedges, K. *The Power of Presence: Unlock Your
    Potential to Influence and Engage Others*,
    American Management Association, 2012. pp.
    89-106.

19. Henig, R. "Looking for the Lie." *New York Times*,
    2006. Retrieved from https://www.nytimes.com/
    2006/02/05/magazine/looking-for-the-lie.html.
    Accessed 20 April 2018.

20. Kent, R. and Read, C. *Acoustic Analysis of Speech, 2nd
    Edition*. Singular Thomson Learning, 2002, p. 130.

21. Kraft, T. and Pressman, S. "Grin and Bear It: The
    Influence of Manipulated Facial Expression
    on the Stress Response." *Psychological Science*,
    2012. vol. 23, no. 11 pp. 1372-1378. doi:
    10/1177/0956797612445312

22. Kragel, P. and LaBar, K. "Somatosensory Representations Link the Perception of Emotional Expressions and Sensory Experience." *Cognition and Behavior,* 2016, vol. 3, no. 2, pp. 1-12. doi: 10.1523/ENEURO.0090-15.2016

23. Levenson, R. and Ruef, A. "Empathy: A Physiological Substrate." *Journal of Personality and Social Psychology,* 1992, vol. 63, no. 2, pp. 234-246.

24. "Listening Facts." *International Listening Association.* n.d. Retrieved from https://www.listen.org/Listening-Facts. Accessed 11 April 2018.

25. Liu, W., et al. "Leader Humility and Team Innovation: Investigating the Substituting Role of Task Interdependence and the Mediating Role of Team Voice Climate." *Frontiers in Psychology,* 2017, vol. 8:1115. doi: 10.3389/fpsyg.2017.01115

26. Netemeyer, R., et al. "Store Manager Performance and Satisfaction: Effects of Store Employee Performance and Satisfaction, Store Customer Satisfaction, and Store Customer Spending Growth." *Journal of Applied Psychology,* 2010, vol. 95, no. 3, pp. 530-545. doi: 10.1037/a0017630

27. "Resonance." *The Physics Classroom,* 2018. Retrieved from http://www.physicsclassroom.com /class/sound/Lesson-5/Resonance. Accessed 7 April 2018.

28. "Resonance." *Oxford Living Dictionaries.* Oxford University Press, 2018. Retrieved from https://en.oxforddictionaries.com/definition /resonance. Accessed 7 April 2018.

29. "Resound." *Merriam-Webster Dictionary.* Merriam Webster, 2018. Retrieved from https://www.merriamwebster.com/ dictionary/resound. Accessed 7 April 2018.

30. Rund, J. *Unequaled: Tips for Building a Successful Career Through Emotional Intelligence,* John Wiley & Sons, 2016, pp. 110-111, 125-138.

31. Ryback, D. *Putting Emotional Intelligence to Work: Successful Leadership is More than IQ,* Butterworth-Heinemann, 1998.

32. van Dierendonck, D. "Servant Leadership: A Review and Synthesis." *Journal of Management,* 2011, vol. 37, no. 4, pp. 1228-1261. doi: 10.1177/0149206310310380462

33. Vianello, M., et al. "Elevation at Work: The Effects of Leaders' Moral Excellence."*Journal of Positive Psychology,* 2010, vol. 5, no. 5, pp. 390-411. doi:10.1080/1743760.2010.516764

34. Wojciszke, B. and Abele, A. "The Primacy of Communion Over Agency and its Reversals in Evaluation." *European Journal of Social Psychology,* 2008, vol. 38, no.7, pp. 1139-1147. doi: 10.1002/ejsp

35. Wojciszke, B., et al. "On the Dominance of Moral Categories on Impression Formation." *Personality and Social Psychology Bulletin,* 1998, vol. 24, no. 12, pp. 1251-1263.

Self-Control

1. Baumeister, R. and Tierney, J. *Rediscovering the Greatest Human Strength: Willpower,* The Penguin Press, 2011.

2. Blair, R. "The Neurobiology of Impulse Aggression." *Journal of Child and Adolescent Psychopharmacology,* 2016, vol. 26, no. 1, pp.4-9 doi: 10/1089/cap.2015.0088

3. Bremmer, R., Koole, S., and Bushman, B. "'Pray for Those Who Mistreat You': Effects of Prayer on Anger and Aggression." *Personality and Social Psychology Bulletin,* 2011, vol. 37, no. 6, pp. 830-837

4. Bushman, B. "Does Venting Anger Feed or Extinguish the Flame? Catharsis, Rumination, Distraction, Anger, and

Aggressive Responding." *Personality and Social Psychology Bulletin*, 2002, vol. 28, no. 6, pp. 724-731

5. Bushman, B., Baumeister, R., and Phillips, C. "Do People Aggress to Improve Their Mood? Catharsis Beliefs, Affect Regulation Opportunity, and Aggressive Responding." *Journal of Personality and Social Psychology*, 2001, vol. 81, no. 1 pp. 17-32 doi: 10.1037//0022-3514.81.1.17

6. Bushman, B. and Whitaker, J. "Like a Magnet: Catharsis Beliefs Attract Angry People to Violent Video Games." *Psychological Science*, 2010, vol. 21, no. 6, pp. 790-792 doi: 10.1177/0956797610369494

7. Chester, D., and DeWall, N. "The Pleasure of Revenge: Retaliatory Aggression Arises From a Neural Imbalance Toward Reward." *Social Cognitive and Affective Neuroscience*, 2015, vol. 11, no. 7, pp. 1173-1182 doi:10.1093/scan/nsv082

8. Cox, D., et al. "The Effect of Anger Expression Style on Cardiovascular Responses to Lateralized Cognitive Stressors." *Brain Informatics*, 2017 doi: 10.1007/s40708-017-0068-4

9. Dambacher, F., et al. "Out of Control: Evidence for Anterior Insula Involvement in Motor Impulsivity and Reactive Aggression." *Social Cognitive and Affective Neuroscience*, 2015, vol.10, pp. 508-516 doi: 10.1093/scan/nsu077

10. de Boer, S., et al. "The Vicious Cycle Towards Violence: Focus on the Negative Feedback Mechanisms of Brain Serotonin Neurotransmission." *Frontiers in Behavioral Neuroscience*, 2009, vol. 3, article 52 doi: 10.3389/neuro.08.052/2009

11. DeWall, N., et al. "A Grateful Heart is a Nonviolent Heart: Cross-Sectional, Experience Sampling, Longitudinal, and Experimental Evidence." *Social Psychological and Personality Science*, 2011, vol. 3, no. 232 doi: 10/1177/1948550611416675

12. Garfinkel, S., et al. "Anger in Brain and Body: The Neural and Physiological Perturbation of Decision-Making by Emotion." *Social Cognitive and Affective Neuroscience*, 2016, vol. 11, no. 1, pp. 150-158 doi: 10.1093/scan/nsv099

13. Goleman, D. *Social Intelligence: The New Science of Human Relationships*, Bantam Dell, 2006.

14. Hoaken, P., Shaughnessy, V., and Pihl, R. "Executive Cognitive Functioning and Aggression: Is it an Issue of Impulsivity?" *Aggressive Behavior*, 2003, vol. 29, pp. 15-30 doi: 10/1002/ab.10023

15. Job, V., et al. "Beliefs About Willpower Determine the Impact of Glucose on Self-Control." *PNAS*, 013, vol. 10, no. 37, pp. 14837-14842 doi: 10.1073/pnas.1313475110

16. Krakowski, M. "Violence and Serotonin: Influence of Impulse Control, Affect Regulation, and Social Functioning." *Journal of Neuropsychiatry and Clinical Neuroscience*, 2003, vol. 15, no. 3, pp. 294-305

17. Saini, M. "A Meta-Analysis of the Psychological Treatment of Anger: Developing Guidelines for Evidence-Based Practice." *Journal of American Academy of Psychiatry Law*, 2009, vol. 37, no. 4, pp. 473-488

18. Skatova, A., et al., "Guilty Repair Sustains Cooperation, Angry Retaliation Destroys It." *Scientific Reports*, 2017 doi: 10/1038/srep46709

19. Tang, Y., et al. "Short-Term Meditation Increases Blood Flow in Anterior Cingulate Cortex and Insula." *Frontiers in Psychology*, 2015, vol. 6 doi: 10.3389/fpsyg.2015.00212

20. Tang, Y., et al. "Short-Term Meditation Induces White Matter Changes in the Anterior Cingulate." *PNAS*, 2010, vol. 107, no. 35, pp. 15649-15652

    doi: 10.1073/pnas.1011043107

21. Tang, Y., et al. "Central and Autonomic Nervous System Interaction is Altered by Short-Term Meditation." *PNAS*, 2009, vol. 106, no. 22, pp. 8865-8870 doi: 10.1073/pnas.0904031106

22. Tangney, J., Baumeister, R., and Boone, A. "High Self Control Predicts Good Adjustment, Less Pathology, Better Grades, and Interpersonal

Success." *Self-Regulation and Self-Control,*
Routledge, 2018, pp. 181-220.

23. Taren, A., et al. "Mindfulness Meditation Training
    Alters Stress-Related Amygdala Resting State
    Functional Connectivity: A Randomized
    Controlled Trial." *Social-Cognitive and
    Affective Neuroscience,* 2015, vol. 10, no. 12,
    pp. 1758-1768

24. Taylor, V., et al. "Impact of Meditation Training in the
    Default Mode Network During a Restful State."
    Social-Cognitive and Affective Neuroscience,
    2012, vol. 8, no. 1 pp. 4-14

25. Thomaes, S., et al. "Turning Shame Inside-Out:
    'Humiliated Fury' in Young Adolescents."
    Emotion, 2011, vol. 11, no. 4, pp. 786-793 doi:
    10.1037/a0023403

26. Wagner, D., and Heatherton, T. "Self-Regulatory
    Depletion Increases Emotional Reactivity in the
    Amygdala." *SCAN,* 2013, vol. 8, pp. 410-417.
    doi:10.1093/scan/nss082

27. Willowski, B., Robinson, M., and Troop-Gordon, W.
    "How Does Cognitive Control Reduce Anger
    and Aggression? The Role of Conflict
    Monitoring and Forgiveness." *Journal of
    Personality and Social Psychology,* 2010, vol.
    98, no. 5, p. 830

28. Veenstra, L., et al. "Drawn to Danger: Trait Anger
    Predicts Automatic Approach Behaviours to
    Angry Faces." *Cognition and Emotion,* 2016,
    vol. 31, no. 4, pp. 765-771 doi:
    10.1080/02699931.2016.1150256

29. Xue, S., Tang, Y., and Posner, M. "Short-term
    Meditation Increases Network Efficiency
    of the Anterior Cingulate Cortex." *Cognitive
    Neuroscience and Neuropsychology,* 2011, vol.
    22, pp. 570-574 doi:
    10.1097/WNR.0b013e328348c750

30. Zhan, J., et al. "Regulatin Anger Under Stress Via
    Cognitive Reappraisal and Sadness."

Frontiers in Psychology, 2017, vol. 8, article
1372 doi: 10.3389/fpsyg.2017.01372

Kindness

1. Abhishekh, H., et al. "Influence of Age and Gender on Autonomic Regulation of the Heart." *Journal of Clinical Monitoring and Computing*, 2013, vol. 27, no. 3 pp. 259-264. Abstract. doi: 10.1007/s10877-012-9424-3

2. Alda, M., et al. "Zen Meditation, Length of Telomeres, and the Role of Experiential Avoidance and Compassion." *Mindfulness*, 2016, vol. 7, pp. 651-659 doi:10/1007/s12671-016-0500-5

3. Blau, H., et al. "The Central Role of Stem Cells in Regenerative Failure with Aging." *Natural Medicine*, vol. 21, no. 8, pp. 854-862 doi:10.1038/nm.3918

4. Brody, G., et al. "Prevention Effects Ameliorate the Prospective Association Between Non-Supportive Parenting and Diminished Telomere Length." *Prevention Science*, 2015, vol. 16, no. 2, pp. 171-180. doi:10.1007/s11121-014-04742

5. Condon, P. and Desbordes, G. "Meditation Increases Compassionate Response to Suffering." *Psychological Science*, 2013, vol. 24, no. 10, pp. 2125-2127. doi: 10.1177/0956797613485603

6. Condon, P. and DeStono, D. "Compassion for One Reduced Punishment for Another." *Journal of Experimental Social Psychology*, 2011, vol. 47, pp. 698-701. doi: 10.1016/j.jesp.2010.11.016

7. "Chréstotés." HELPS Word-studies. 2011. Retrieved from *BibleHub*, https://biblehub.com/greek/5544.htm

8. DeMeersman, R. and Stein, P. "Vagal Modulation and Aging." *Biological Psychology*, 2007, vol.74, pp. 165-173. doi:10.1016/j.biopsycho.2006.04.008

9. Elabd, C., et al. "Oxytocin is an Age-Specific Circulating Hormone that is Necessary for

Muscle Maintenance and Regeneration."*Nature Communications*. 2014. doi:10/1038/ncomms5082

10. Epel, E., et al. "Can Meditation Slow Rate of Cellular Aging? Cognitive Stress, Mindfulness,and Telomeres." *Annals of the New York Academy of Sciences,* 2009, vol. 1172, no. 1, pp. 34-53 doi: 10/1111/j.17496632.04414.x.

11. Fabes, R., et al. "The Effects of Young Children's Affiliations with Prosocial Peers on Subsequent Emotionality in Peer Interactions." *British Journal of Developmental Psychology,* 2012, vol. 30, no. 4, pp. 569-585 doi: 10.1111/j.2044835X/2011. 02073.x.

12. Floyd, K. "Human Affection Exchange: XII. Affectionate Communication is Associated with Diurnal Variation in Salivary Free Cortisol." *Western Journal of Communication,* 2006, vol. 70, no. 1, pp. 47-63 doi: 10.1080/10570310500506649

13. Floyd, K., et al. "Human Affection Exchange: XIV. Relationship Affection Predicts Resting Heart Rate and Free Cortisol Secretion During Acute Stress." *Behavioral Medicine,* 2007, vol. 32, pp. 151-156.

14. Hamilton, D. *The Five Side Effects of Kindness,* Hay House, 2017.

15. Harper, Douglas. "Kindness." *Online Etymology Dictionary,* 2018. Retrieved from https://www.etymonline.com/word/kind. Accessed 26 April 2018.

16. Heinrichs, M., et al. "Oxytocin, Vasopressin, and Human Social Behavior." *Frontiers in Neuroendocrinology.* 2009, vol. 30, pp. 548 557. doi: 10.1016/j.yfrne.2009.05.005

17. Hotta, H., and Uchida, S. "Aging of the Autonomic Nervous System and Possible Improvements in Autonomic Activity Using Somatic Afferent Stimulation." *Geriatrics and Geronotology*

International, 2010, vol. 10, supplement 1, pp. S127-S136. doi: 10.1111/j.1447 0594.2010.00592.x

18. Ignarro, L. Quote retrieved from https://proargibenefits.files.wordpress.com/ 2009/11/quotes-on-l-arginine-lrk.pdf. Accessed 27 April 2018.

19. Jankowski, M., et al. "Oxytocin in the Heart Regeneration." *Recent Patents on Cardiovascular Drug Discovery,* 2012, vol. 7, pp. 81-87.

20. Vine, W.E., et al. "Kindness." *Vine's Complete Expository Dictionary of Old and New Testament Words.* Thomas Nelson, Inc., 1996.

21. Light, K., et al. "More Frequent Partner Huge and Higher Oxytocin Levels are Linked to Lower Blood Pressure and Heart Rate in Premenopausal Women." *Biological Psychology,* 2004, 69, pp. 5-21 doi: 10.1016/j.biopsycho.2004.11.002

22. "Metanoia." *Strong's Exhaustive Concordance Updated Edition.* Retrieved from *BibleHub.* https://biblehub.com/greek/3341.htm

23. McLaughlin, K., et al. "Low Vagal Tone Magnifies the Association Between Psychosocial Stress Exposure and Internalizing Psychopathology in Adolescents." *Journal of Clinical Child and Adolescent Psychology,* 2015, vol. 44, no. 2, pp. 314-328. doi:10.1080/15374416.2013.843464

24. Mikolajczak, M., et al. "Oxytocin Makes People Trusting, Not Gullible." *Psychological Science.* 2010, vol. 21, no. 8, pp. 1072-1074 doi: 10.1177/0956797610377343

25. Mongrain, M, and Shapira, L. "Practicing Compassion Increases Happiness and Self-Esteem." *Journal of Happiness Studies,* 2011, doi: 10.1007/s10902-010-9239-1

26. "Nitric Oxide." *Encyclopaedia Britanica,* Encyclopaedia Britanica, Inc., 2018. Retrieved

from https://www.britannica.com/science/nitric-oxide. Accessed 27 April 2018.

27. Over, H. and Carpenter, M. "Eighteen-Month-Old Infants Show Increased Helping Following Priming with Affiliation." *Psychological Science,* 2009, vol. 20, no. 10, pp. 1189-1193. doi: 10.1111/j/1467-9280.2009.02419.x

28. "Philanthrópia." *Strong's Exhaustive Concordance Updated Edition.* Retrieved from *BibleHub.* https://biblehub.com/greek/5363.htm

29. Rein, G., et al. "The Physiological and Psychological Effects of Compassion and Anger." *Journal of Advancement in Medicine,* 1995, vol. 8, no. 2, pp. 87-105.

30. Shammas, M. "Telomeres, Lifestyle, Cancer, and Aging." *Current Opinion in Clinical Nutrition and Metabolic Care,* 2011, vol. 14, no. 1, pp. 28-34. doi: 10.1097/MCO.0b013e32834121b1

31. "The Facts About Sarcopenia." *Aging in Motion,* Alliance for Aging Research, n.d. Retrieved from http://www.aginginmotion.org/wp content/uploads/2011/04/sarco penia_fact sheet.pdf. Accessed 27 April 2018.

32. Thimmapuram, J., et al. "Effect of Heartfulness Meditation on Burnout, Emotional Wellness,and Telomere Length in Health Care Professionals." *Journal of Community Hospital Internal Medicine Perspectives,* 2017, vol. 7, no. 3, pp. 21-27 doi:10.1080/20009666.2016.1270806

Humility

1. Collins, J. "Level 5 Leadership: The Triumph of Humility and Emotional Resolve." *Harvard Business Review,* 2001, pp. 66-76. Retrieved from file:///F:/Research%20documents/Humility/Level5%20Leadership%20Jim%20Collins.pdf

2. Farrell, J., et al. "Humility and Relationship Outcomes in Couples." *Couple and Family Psychology:Research and Practice.* 2015, vol. 4, no. 1, pp.14-26. doi:10.1037/cfp0000033

3. Johnson, M., et al. "A New Trait on the Market: Honesty-Humility as a Unique Predictor of Job Performance Ratings." *Personality and Individual Differences,* 2011, vol. 50, pp. 857-862. doi: 10.1177/009164711404200111

4. Kruse, E., et al. "An Upward Spiral Between Gratitude and Humility." *Social Psychological and Personality Science,* 2014, vol. 5, no. 7, pp. 805-814. doi: 10.1177/1948550614534700

5. Morris, J., et al. "Bringing Humility to Leadership: Antecedents and and Consequences of Leadership Humility." *Human Relations,* 2005, vol. 58, no. 10, pp. 1323-1350. doi:10.1177/0018726705059929

6. Peters, A., et al. "Associations Between Dispositional Humility and Social Relationship Quality." *Psychology,* 2011, vol. 2, no. 3, pp. 155-161. doi: 10.4236/psych.2011.23025

7. "Prautés." HELPS Word-studies. 2011. Retrieved from *BibleHub,* https://biblehub.com/greek/4240.htm

8. "Tapeinophrosune." HELPS Word-studies. 2011. Retrieved from *BibleHub,* https://biblehub.com/greek/5012.htm

9. Tong, E., et al. "Humility Facilitates Higher Self-Control." *Journal of Experimental Social Psychology,* 2016, vol. 62, pp. 30-39. doi: 10.1016/j.jesp.2015.09.008

10. Van Tongeren, D., et al. "Humility Attenuates Negative Attitudes and Behaviors Toward Religious Out Group Members." *The Journal of Positive Psychology,* 2016, vol.11, no. 2, pp. 199-208. doi: 10.1080/17439760.2015.1037861

11. Vine, W.E., et al. "Humble." *Vine's Complete Expository Dictionary of Old and New Testament Words.* Thomas Nelson, Inc., 1996.

12. Vine, W.E., et al. "Humbleness of Mind, Humility." *Vine's Complete Expository Dictionary of Old and New Testament Words.* Thomas Nelson, Inc., 1996.

Grace

1. Benner, J. "The Meaning of Grace from a Hebrew Perspective." Ancient Hebrew Research Center, https://www.ancient-hebrew.org/studies words/meaning-of-grace-from-a-hebrew-perspective.htm

2. Bufford, R., et al. "Dimensions of Grace." *Faculty Publications–Graduate School of Clinical Psychology*, 2013, paper 86, http://digitalcommons.georgefox.edu /gscp_fac/86

3. Bufford, R., et al. "Dimensions of Grace: Factor Analysis of Three Grace Scales." *Psychology of Religion and Spirituality*, 2016, http://dx.doi.org/10.1037/rel0000064

4. Bufford,R., et al. "Measuring Grace: Further Development and Validation of a Grace Measure." *Faculty Publications–Graduate School of Clinical Psychology*,2013, paper 6. http://digitalcommons.georgefox.edu/gscp_fac/6

5. Bufford, R. & McGinn, M. "The Effects of Grace Interventions in Church Communities." *The Journal of Positive Psychology*, 2017, doi: 10.1080/17439760.2017.1350740

6. "Charis." HELPS Word-Studies. 2011. Retrieved from *BibleHub*, https://biblehub.com/greek/5485.htm

7. "Chen." HELPS Word-Studies. 2011. Retrieved from *BibleHub*, https://biblehub.com/hebrew/2580.htm

8. "Chesed." *Brown-Driver-Briggs Hebrew and English Lexicon*. BibleSoft, Inc. 2006. Retrieved from *BibleHub*, https://biblehub.com/hebrew/2617.htm

9. "En." HELPS Word-Studies. 2011. Retrieved from *BibleHub*, https://biblehub.com/greek/1722.htm

10. "Favor." *Merriam-Webster*. 2018, https://www.merriamwebster.com/dictionary/favor. Accessed 25 September, 2019.

11. Geczy-Haskins, L. "The Effects of Grace on Self forgiveness in a Religious Community." 2017. George Fox University, PsyD dissertation. http://digitalcommons.georgefox.edu/psyd/216

12. "Grace." *Merriam-Webster.* 2018,
    https://www.merriamwebster.com/dictionary
    /grace Accessed 25 September, 2019.

13. Moody, J. "The Effects of a Grace Intervention in a
    Christian Congregation: A Study of
    Positive Psychology in the Church." 2015.
    George Fox University, PsyD dissertation.
    http://digitalcommons.georgefox.edu/psyd/194

14. "Techinnah." HELPS Word-Studies. 2011. Retrieved
    from *BibleHub,*
    https://biblehub.com/hebrew/8467.htm

15. Snaith, N. "The Meaning of Chesed." *Distinctive Ideas
    of the Old Testament,* London, 1944. As cited
    on http://www.bibleresearcher.com/chesed.html

16. Watson, P. "Sin and Self-Functioning, Part 1: Grace,
    Guilt, and Self-Consciousness." *Journal of
    Psychology and Theology,* 1988, vol. 16, no. 3,
    pp. 254-69. doi: 10.1177/009164718801600305

Social Connection

1. Coan, J., et al. "Lending a Hand." *Psychological
    Science,* 2006, vol. 17, no. 12, pp. 1032-1039.

2. Ertelt, S. "Their 'Rescuing Hug' Stunned the World,
    Now the Twins are All Grown Up." *LifeNews,*
    20 June 2014. Retrieved from
    http://www.lifenews.com/2014/06/20/
    their-rescuing-hug-stunned-the-world-now-the
    twins-are-all-grown-up/.Accessed 24 May 2018.

3. Feldman, R., Rosenthal, Z., and Eidelman, A. "Maternal
    Preterm Skin-to-Skin Contact Enhances Child
    Physiologic Organization and Cognitive Control
    Across the First 10 Years of Life." *Biological
    Psychiatry,* 2014, vol. 75, no. 1 doi:
    10.1016/j.biopsych.2013.08.012

4. Flacking, R., et al. "Closeness and Separation in
    Neonatal Intensive Care." *Acta Paediatrica*

(Oslo, Norway:1992), 2012, vol. 101, no. 10, pp. 1032-1037.doi:10.1111/j.1651-2227.2012.02787.

5. Floyd, K., et al. "Human Affection Exchange: XIV. Relationship Affection Predicts Resting Heart Rate and Free Cortisol Secretion During Acute Stress." *Behavioral Medicine*, 2007, vol. 32, pp. 151-156.

6. Lamm, C. and Singer, T. "The Role of Anterior Insular Cortex in Social Emotions." *Brain Structure and Function*, 2010, 214: 5-6, pp. 579-591 doi:10.1007/s00429-010-0251-3

7. Light, K., et al. "More Frequent Partner Huge and Higher Oxytocin Levels are Linked to Lower Blood Pressure and Heart Rate in Premenopausal Women." *Biological Psychology*, 2004, 69, pp. 5-21 doi: 10.1016/j.biopsycho.2004.11.002

8. Lyubomirsky, S. *The How of Happiness*, The Penguin Press, 2008, pp. 140-159.

9. Lyubomirsky, S. *The Myths of Happiness*, The Penguin Press, 2013, pp. 43-46.

10. Rein, G., et al. "The Physiological and Psychological Effects of Compassion and Anger." *Journal of Advancement in Medicine*,1995, vol. 8, no. 2, pp. 87-105.

11. Rolls, E. "The Orbitofrontal Cortex and Reward." *Cerebral Cortex*, 2000, vol. 10, pp. 284-294.

www.ingramcontent.com/pod-product-compliance
Lightning Source LLC
Chambersburg PA
CBHW051425090426
42737CB00014B/2830